GLOBETROTS

Stephen Kanold

HAVANA BOOK GROUP LLC
HAVANABOOKGROUP.COM

No part of this publication may be reproduced, stored in a retrieval system, or transmitted in any form or by any means – electronic, mechanical, photocopying, recording or otherwise – without the written permission of the publisher.

HAVANA BOOK GROUP LLC

43537 RIDGE PARK DRIVE

TEMECULA, CA. 92590

COPYRIGHT 2021 All rights reserved.

ISBN: 978-1-7353117-2-2

(Original cover concept design by Dixie Kanold)

FOREWORD

"*Globetrots* will take you on a humorous yet realistic journey narrated with wit, adventure, and experience. Steve Kanold shares insight about his life as a tour operator who has traversed the world several times over with his often, "impossible to please" American clients. After reading *Globetrots*, I would travel with him and his partner Lalo Alvarez at a minute's notice." -- "Francoise Rhodes, *Traveling with Francois*, television, videocasts and travel blogger.

CHAPTER OVERVIEW

INTRODUCTION..vii

Chapter 1 - GLOBETROTS..xv

Chapter 2 - EUROPE...15

Chapter 3 - ASIA...45

Chapter 4 - AFRICA & THE MIDDLE EAST...65

Chapter 5 - AUSTRALIA, NEW ZEALAND, & OCEANIA..................................85

Chapter 6 - CENTRAL & SOUTH AMERICA...101

Chapter 7 - ANTARCTICA..121

Chapter 8 - EXOTIC DESTINATIONS...129

Chapter 9 - NOT HAVANA GOOD TIME..143

Chapter 10 - THOUGHTS SUITABLE FOR POSTCARDS..................................153

EPILOGUE..177

INTRODUCTION

Complaining not only ruins everyone else's day, it ruins the complainer's day, too. The more we complain the more unhappy we get. —**Dennis Prager**

More than 45 years ago, in the bucolic San Bernardino County town of Bloomington, California, I customized my first overseas group tour. The travelers consisted of German language high schoolers—*my* students, to be precise—and a handful of adult chaperones. Why learn the language, I figured, if you can't use it? Off to Germanic countries in Europe we went.

My *Sudeten* were placed for a week at the homes of German friends and relatives in Bremen, where they were forced to speak the language. Accommodations for the chaperones were at a hillside chalet situated in a forest, so that while the kids were away the adults played, or as one escort described it, the hills were alive with the sound of drunks. (Back in America, the reputation of a party trip must have spread, because twice as many chaperones signed up for the tour three years later).

Each passing decade featured more group travel, until finally in 1991 I was asked by the Palm Springs Unified School District to create a "Global Classroom" for its Adult School. The rules were simple: make the trips educational, i.e. no forays to Disneyland;

mail informative newsletters before each tour; stage documentation meetings; submit comprehensive lesson plans with goals, and above all, have participants--who were mostly retired seniors--sign liability waivers before leaving U.S. soil.

I partnered with a friend and fellow businessman, Lalo Alvarez, who also had traveled extensively. Together we researched in advance the hotels, sites, and amenities of each city and country. Unlike many travel agents, who haven't ventured east of Las Vegas, the two of us still preview beforehand most of the destinations that we offer to the public.

Trips to Italy, France, Greece, Germany, Switzerland, China, and the Panama Canal were sold through the Adult School, primarily to Coachella Valley residents. Not one complaint was lodged. So, when the district's superintendent called me into his office one day and announced he was pulling the plug on the program, I was dismayed and surprised. What had gone wrong?

"Not a thing," he answered. "In fact, only raves about the travel program have been reported to us. The issue is this: Our fear is that one day a senior citizen will topple off the Great Wall of China with his Brownie camera and the district will be sued. Steve, we don't even allow field trips anymore, including to our local library. On the way there, some kid might trip over a lawn spigot."

I stammered, "But the district is holding more than $70,000 of clients' money. Many consider their holiday with us the trip of a lifetime."

"Return their deposits," the superintendent said standing up, indicating the conversation was over. "Write and mail them a letter. As of today, Adult School Travel ceases to exist."

Within 72 hours, I had 1) applied for a business license using the name Adult Customized Tours Inc. (we decided to keep "Adult" in the name, as it was recognized by the community), 2) opened a client trust account per California law, and 3) had our new company insured. I sent out a letter explaining the district's decision and informed everyone that they could either receive a full refund or have monies moved to A.C.T., which would operate the same programs. My heart sang when not one person asked for a refund—*all 92 Adult School Travel participants transferred their funds to A.C.T.!* Even now, I am touched by the loyalty of those founding travelers. The same tenets demanded by the school district in 1991 (pre-tour newsletters, meetings, personal service) are intact today.

That is the genesis of Adult Customized Tours, popularly known as A.C.T., established in January 1995. What follows on these pages is not a travelogue as one would normally expect, i.e. a guide book which details histories of places and presents directions to sites and restaurants. An Arthur Frommer or Rick Steve's book this is not; instead, revealed herein are insights and stories from me, a licensed tour operator, who is not to be confused with a travel agent, who typically caters to individuals. People don't visit our office to purchase plane tickets to Fresno. In fact, A.C.T. often sells its group vacations to travel agencies, who add a commission to their rates.

Contained in this book is a mixed bag of impressions describing both good and bad travelers over the years, people I've tried to portray lightheartedly (God forbid you think I'm simply complaining about complainers!).* The playful subtitle, "A seasoned tour operator tells whining American travelers where to go" is not misleading, as the book actually contains many suggestions of where to go and what to expect within countries outside of the United States. So, lean back in your easy chair, kick off your shoes, pour yourself a glass of French or Chilean wine, use your passport as a coaster and savor this sentimental journey down Memory Lane!

*A sense of humor, the most important thing one can pack, will render calamities suffered abroad inconsequential. "Live, love, and laugh" should be every traveler's philosophy.

Our first customized tour: Bloomington High School students stand before the Roland Statue in Bremen, 1976. I am the 25-year-old teacher wearing lederhosen shorts in the front row.

GLOBETROTS

But why, oh why, do the wrong people travel when the right people stay at home?

- Noel Coward

After five decades of international travel with Americans

(30 years of them in the role of licensed tour operator) to over a hundred Republics, Emirates, Democratic Unions, Sultanates, Kingdoms, Principalities, United whatevers, territories, island nations, city states, and countries like Romania and Paraguay that are just in the way of others; and after seeing Yankees tiptoe past hotel guards armed with submachine guns in Israel and dining together aboard umpteen luxury cruise ships and stepping into human feces at Varanasi on the Ganges River and getting pawed at by beggars in similar shit holes of the world, I have news to report on the home front: Americans often—but not always--make lousy tourists.

My belly churns at the memories of stupid behavior from the Chesters, Sylvias, Herberts, Bettys, and Eugenes who have journeyed with me beyond the secure borders of the U.S.A. With names like those, senior citizens are the subjects at hand, people 65 years and older who are off to see the world in their sunset years, believing there is such a lot of world to see. Would that they see it on the Travel Channel....

Call it *globetrots,* this malady that makes me dash to the toilet at the reminiscence of the scowling octogenarian who, on a beautiful day in Portofino, Italy, blames me, his travel agent, for failing to tell him to pack sun shorts. Or the cranky woman on the bus who yells to her learned guide in Xian, China, "How much longer before we get to the Teriyaki soldiers?" Globetrots strikes when Americans whine about how lasagna in Italy is not as good as that at Olive Garden Restaurant, or when they gripe about the lack of griddle cakes and smoky links on the breakfast menu in Rangoon.

"You didn't tell me there'd be walking on this tour!" cries an obese lady from Palm Springs, who fails to understand why her touring coach cannot drive directly into Red Square.

Maybe because they have it so good in the United States, with so many comforts, that even a week spent on international soil sends Americans into a state of panic. They are not truly happy until they return from their vacation. In anticipation of a holiday, they become tense and implode, often canceling their tour because of frayed nerves and then blaming everyone but themselves for the subsequent financial penalty. While abroad, they are so on guard (a good state to be in, actually) that they find it difficult if not impossible to relax. This is ironic, because the word *vacation,* from the Latin word *vacatio* meaning "to release, to vacate," should have the opposite effect. Only after they return to their natural surroundings on Main Street U.S.A. do these Americans realize they enjoyed their trip, and not until they view their photos do they appreciate all they experienced. Their exhilaration on being home has less to do with having seen a lion on safari in Africa than it does with the sense that at their age, they *survived* the trip.

The day before departure may be the toughest for many Americans. For months they anticipate their Great Getaway, their Dream Vacation, and (to many) their Romantic Interlude in a foreign land. They count down the days before the trip like mission control at Houston Space Center; from the early planning stages they are aware of the departure date, that proverbial train, heading toward them. Trouble is, they can't seem to get off the tracks. Either their packing has not gone right, or--from neurosis--an illness has set in, or the stock market has crashed and suddenly affordability becomes an issue. There is always a reason for last-minute calamities, which then result in loss of sleep.

Not getting a good night's rest before a long flight can be the chief reason why Americans arrive sick in foreign countries. Their bodies are simply worn out from worry and tiredness, making them prone to any number of viruses circulating through the plane's air ducts. Their weak immune systems are further hampered when they drink alcohol, ostensibly to "begin the party" or to calm their frazzled nerves. Because most passengers are unable to sleep soundly while flying (especially those seated in economy class), that first day without rest grows into two. This is tough enough on young people, but with seniors, the results can be life threatening. More than once we have had to arrange for travelers to return home early, because of illness brought on by lack of rest.

The solution is obvious: people should make a list of things to do in advance and check them off days before their vacation begins. They should *force* themselves—even if they are night owls—to go to bed early prior to departing on a long flight, and if it is scheduled in the morning and they do not live near the airport, they should open their wallets and pay for a hotel room! It never ceases to amaze me how people will fork out thousands of dollars for a holiday and be tight when it comes to important matters like spending the night at an airport hotel. Many decide to leave their homes at 3 a.m. (meaning they arise at around 2 a.m.) to be at the airport by dawn for their flight three hours later. Fifteen hours afterward, when their plane finally lands in Greece, they salute the birthplace of Western civilization by puking on the tarmac.

More millionaires have been on our tours than I care to count, and the majority of them fly in coach. When traveling long distances to places like Africa and Asia, why would one in that financial bracket *not* spring for a business class seat? Barbara Hutton once observed, "I've never seen a Brinks truck follow a hearse to the cemetery," but apparently some people intend to take it with them. I say, *if you can afford it, treat yourself to a seat upgrade on your flights*—not only will you arrive rested with your luggage in tow (upgraded seats include priority baggage handling), but the amenities, including business and first-class lounges at the airport, actually give you something to look forward to at the beginning and end of your vacation.

The state of being ill-prepared before a trip, as well as whining, blaming, and uneasiness while abroad, is uniquely American. One seldom sees European or Asian tourists crying into their Pabst Blue Ribbon when they come to our shores. If their touring bus breaks down, you don't hear them cursing at the guide or catch them sulking. I'll never forget a woman who, when our Mercedes bus broke a fan belt outside of Naples, Italy, causing a delay in catching the ferry to the island of Capri, blamed *me* for her missing out on the Blue Grotto.

"What did I have to do with the fan belt breaking?" I asked her.

She snapped, "By the time we arrived, the sea was too high to enter the Grotto; you should have planned on these things and checked the tide chart before we left home."

*Blaming one's travel agent for every mishap abroad has become an American pastime. A freak rainstorm in New Zealand during summer? The agent's fault. Food poisoning on the Nile cruise in Egypt? It could not have been the mayonnaise dressing you were warned to avoid but ate anyway; the tour company is to be blamed for choosing the wrong boat. Wallets are stolen by pickpockets at the Roman Trevi Fountain—where was the escort to protect us? A woman on one of our tours once willingly spent over $200 on herbal medicine in Beijing, and two weeks later demanded a refund in Shanghai. "You took us there," she said angrily to me. "I want a refund, because I wouldn't have bought it if your company hadn't stopped there."

When it comes to mishaps on a trip, it is never an act of God (i.e., inclement weather), machinery (snapped fan belts), or fate (being robbed). It is always the fault of the agent of travel, to whom payment was given. When playing the Blame Game, don't even *suggest* that the consumer, airline, hotel, or anything else remotely connected to the tour bears responsibility because after all, it was the travel agency *who got the money, who should have watched out for us.*

Foreigners may have their peculiarities (more on that later), but after escorting them on a number of tours inside the U.S., complaining while on vacation is not one of them. They are appreciative, curious, and savvy, which is to say they research destinations before leaving their countries. Unlike most Americans, they take copious notes on board the bus when their guide, to whom they listen intently, speaks. In addition to traveling for pleasure, foreign visitors go to *learn*, while Americans travel to…well, shop.

Many years ago, a friend named Parker, who had lived in Spain, escorted a group of ours to that country's Costa del Sol region. Parker relished the idea of sharing the colorful history of southern Spain with his entourage, from the architectural and cultural influences of the Moors to the history of places like the Alhambra Palace. Being an

educator, he brushed up on all his facts before the trip, and with great anticipation departed the U.S. with his charges. When he returned two weeks later, Parker was disillusioned. "They had no interest at all in my lectures," he lamented. "The three most important things to them were shopping, mealtimes, and hotel accommodations."

He got that right. In Singapore, for example, it has been my experience that Americans prefer to skip the not-to-be-missed Sentosa History Museum in favor of shopping at the duty-free stores on Orchard Road. And who wants extended time to see additional treasures of the Louvre Museum in Paris when you can shop for replicas of them at the Port de Saint Antoine flea market? In Venice, the church in St. Mark's Square is just another basilica—the glass factories are of more interest. Shopping is what Americans want, and if tour operators leave that out of the equation, if they do not allot plenty of time for "commission stops" at factories and local handicraft centers, people complain. (You are probably thinking right now, "No, no, no! I'm not a shopper—how can he accuse me of being one of *those*?" Trust me, you are.)

As Parker observed, equally important is food, which is not to be confused with fine dining. Before signing up for a tour, seniors count the exact number of meals included on the itinerary. While abroad, they constantly need to be apprised of details like what time they eat and for some, where the nearest McDonald's is located. Little wonder that cruising represents the fastest growing segment of the travel industry. Guests on cruise ships can gorge up to 10 times a day. I have seen more than one client excuse himself from dinner after sampling three desserts, only to spot him in line at the midnight buffet just two hours later.

"This is my 44th cruise!" people with asses the size of Texas boast.

"Can you believe it?"

Yes, I can.

The other thing American seniors insist on is what they call "a nice hotel." Confused about the differences between two, three, and four-star properties, but sensing that it was a five-star hotel whose revolving door Princess Diana and Dodi passed through on their last night together, seniors will tell you that a "nice hotel" means one with a private bathroom and the amenities we have at home, like curtains that match the bedspreads, face cloths, bars of soap (rather than the cost-saving liquid stuff), little bottles of shampoo and hair conditioner, and hand moisturizer that on holidays usually lubricate everything but the hands. Never mind lodging at quaint B&B establishments in Europe, where one can really get a taste of local charm or capturing history with an overnight castle stay (they lack elevators and room service). *It is the Holiday Inn Americans want!* Water there is safe to drink, and more than pumpernickel and Swiss cheese await guests at the morning breakfast table: there is an omelet bar, drinkable coffee, and Danish pastries!

In short, the comforts and conveniences Americans enjoy in the States are what they want, what they *expect* in foreign lands. *Don't tell me meatballs were concocted in America—I didn't come all the way to Italy to eat spaghetti without them! Same with egg foo-yung in China. And why does this hotel only have CNN and not offer Fox News? Speaking of hotels, for $49 I can get a better room in Las Vegas, one with a California king bed, than I can for $400 in Iceland. Is there a reason why I can't find even one store in Hanoi that sells* USA Today?

Globetrots.

Let's journey out of North America to each of the six other continents on Earth and see how tourists from the U.S.A. react to them when plucked from their homes and placed there. I'll throw in my two cents about the natives living in these foreign lands, and occasionally comment on the sites that get Americans excited enough to pay big bucks to go there.

Oh, and one thing should be made clear right now, something that is totally obvious: *everything* I say is my opinion, based on observations in my role as a tour operator. You won't find the two words, "I think" or "I believe" in this tome, because anytime someone communicates, that is apparent. When you say, for example, "The weather is warm today," you are really saying, "I think the weather is warm today," or

"In my opinion, the weather is warm today." More to the point, "*It is my experience* that the weather today is warm." It may be cool outside to someone else, but to you, it is warm. So, when I point out traits of the absolute worst travelers, don't react with, "How can he say that?!" It is *my opinion,* after escorting young and old all over the world.

Common traits of these bad apples include rushing to the bus before others to secure the front section, moaning about the location of orchestra seats at theaters, and complaining about virtually *every* aspect of a vacation, from the airline food, cruise ships and hotels, service, weather, guides and escorts, temperature on the motor coach, foreigners, other guests on the tour, prices, and the pervasive smell of tobacco (how many times have I heard "I'm allergic to smoke" from seniors who somehow escaped this allergy in the 1940's, 50's, 60's, and 70's? How did they ever survive those decades?).

Americans stricken with globetrots don't hesitate to vocalize their unhappiness in offensive language, either. "Turn off that Nazi music!" one woman snapped at our bus driver, who had slipped in a tape of happy Bavarian polkas while we were in Germany. The jaws of fellow travelers on the coach dropped in disgust.

Most people gather fond memories while on vacation; travelers with globetrots keep tabs on what goes *wrong*, or what they find repugnant. And they hold on to their misery for the duration of the trip, often spoiling the holiday for others. To prevent that from happening, guides are trained to be polite but firm when confronted by these complainers, who are either at their throats or at their feet. Tour managers and operators speak about them in hushed, off-the-record voices.

Political correctness be damned. It is only out of self control—something so many of them lack—that we in the business refrain from telling these negative souls to simply shut up. If I were to do it over again, my company would be called Optimists-Are-Us Tours & Cruises.

And yes, Virginia, there are **plenty** *of interpretations of who suffers from globetrots on trips, and to every generalization contained herein, for that matter.*

So much for venting. Now that the groundwork has been established, it is time to begin our journey by visiting America's favorite boutique, Europe.

HOPING GUARDIAN ANGELS LEAD ME TO OUR BUS IN ROME

"WHEN THE WALKING TOUR ENDS, HEAD TO THE ASSOS!"
ATHENS, GREECE

COVERING MY EXPOSED LEGS WITH A TABLECLOTH AT THE ENTRANCE TO THE CHURCH OF THE NATIVITY IN BETHLEHAM, PALESTINE. LESSON LEARNED!

(DON'T WEAR SHORTS BY HOLY SITES)

NOT THE NAME OF A TOPLESS BAR, BUT OF NEFERTITI'S FINAL RESTING PLACE.

LUXOR

ROLL WITH IT, STEVE! EXITING A MADAGASCAR POWDER ROOM

EUROPE

Does this boat go to Europe, France?

- Anita Loos, 1888-1981

Ever since currency in Europe went the way of the Euro (a decision many there now regret), the continent has become almost unaffordable to Americans. Those once yummy $1.50 crepes sold on the sidewalks of Paris currently go for about five bucks, and a pizza in Venice will set you back a car payment. Don't even talk about Scandinavia, which has always been pricey due to high social taxes imposed on all non-essential things like restaurants, clothes, and fun. Seeing Europe by ship has become more practical in the new millennium, because at least meals are included in the price (premium onboard eateries notwithstanding), and instead of doling out $9 for a pint at a London pub, a bottle of beer aboard a cruise ship costs about $4, including 15% gratuity to the Philippine waiter.

Seeing the world through a porthole certainly has its advantages. I can honestly report that I have *never* been on a truly <u>bad</u> cruise. Ever! Oh sure, some itineraries have been more interesting than others, and certain vessels have had more allure, luxury, and amenities, but other than that, the cruises were fairly similar. Meals on all liners generally taste the same, i.e., somewhat bland, as they must be seasoned to suit everyone's taste (don't look for curry dishes, Texas chili, or General Tso's spicy chicken on the Love Boat). Service is usually good on all ships, and unless you buy into garden villas or similar expensive accommodations on the newer vessels, even staterooms are alike. But we are digressing from our subject, which is Europe.

Two words sum up disappointment for Americans when it comes to travel, in Europe especially: great expectations. First-timers across The Pond envision the glamour and scenery depicted in travel posters and in Hollywood films. Take the classic 1955 movie, *Summertime*, set in Venice and starring Katherine Hepburn as a spinster who falls in love with shopkeeper Rossano Brazzi. On screen, Venice is painted as a fairly uncrowded fantasyland of gondolas and romantic squares, sprinkled (as opposed to swarming) with happy tourists and precocious but lovable Italian children. Boutique hotels abound, boasting views of the Grand Canal from every window. Anything less than this would disappoint first time visitors from the U.S., who to this day seek out the red wine goblets Kate bought in Brazzi's store.

The reality? In a word, Venice is "choked" with tourists who sometimes have to wait just to pass each other in the maze of narrow corridors snaking through the city. At all times there are so many people visiting this "Jewel of the Adriatic" that the weary Venetians have posted signs on just about every building, pointing the way to Saint Mark's Square for disoriented tourists.

It is hard to name a country in Europe which has *not* been romanticized by the media (Greece in *Mama Mia* comes to mind, and in 2006 Kazakhstan was lampooned in the 2006 movie, *Borat*. Tourism to that eastern European country had reportedly increased 200% soon after the movie was released). Blue skies, little traffic, lush parks, historical ruins—all these promotional images serve as bait to attract the fish. How many times have we seen on television that sexy young couple dancing alone at sunset on the deck of a cruise ship, only later to discover the truth—ubiquitous seniors asking cruise personnel the way back to their cabins? Broadcast on French television are Disney characters beckoning viewers to join them on a tourist-free Main Street at Euro Disneyland. If only that were true…. Here's a reality check for anyone traveling to Europe for the first time:

Park 'n Walk

Buses (we in the travel business refer to them as "motor coaches" in an effort to sound classy) are not allowed to park near ancient monuments in Europe, for a variety of reasons. At the Coliseum in Rome, for example, traffic around the site has threatened the foundations, so now coaches must park up to a quarter of a mile away, much to the dismay of American seniors. Same is true with the Leaning Tower of Pisa—you wouldn't want your bus to be the fault of it finally collapsing, would you? (If that should occur, blame the tour company, whose guide should have known where to park).

Security all over the world has tightened, of course, further adding restrictions to parking near monuments and government buildings. Accessibility is another factor. Not to pick on Italy, but Venice, Portofino, and Siena are cities where buses are either prohibited altogether or limited to distant parking areas. Everyone loves the beautiful medieval village of Saint Paul de Vence in the South of

France, but coaches cannot fit through the narrow cobblestone streets and are not even allowed to drop passengers off at the entrance; people must walk.

uphill from the lot, a hundred yards away. Almost 2000 miles away, in Ephesus, Turkey, the walk is downhill.

LALO IN EPHESUS, TURKEY

In Europe, more than any other continent, parking is a major problem, especially in the big cities and in southern countries, where Italians position their Fiats on sidewalks when there is no other space.

The typical reaction from Americans when told by their guide that they must walk to the Plaka shopping district in Athens, or to Blarney Castle in Ireland, or to Old Town in Bratislava, is, "How far?" or "Why can't the driver just drop us off and be gone?" Before hearing the obvious answer, they turn to their escort or Tour Manager and again accuse him of not telling them in advance there would be walking on the tour. Earth to those afflicted with globetrots now you know—walking in Europe *is* required.

Who Picked Out This Hotel?

Depending on your taste, beds in Europe are either divine or horrific. On the plus side are so-called "feather beds," featuring those snuggly comforters popular in Switzerland and northern countries (excluding Great Britain). Most people melt when they pour into featherbeds, especially if the outside temperature is cold, which it is, typically, in those regions.

On the negative side are the actual sizes of beds in Europe. Even if you stay at one of the bigger chain hotels, king sleepers are almost non-existent. Generally, guests are offered two twins or one double (or a queen if they're lucky). The worst beds are in Italy, where even at pricey establishments it is common to find oneself on a folding, cot-like thing. Don't ask me why Italy can't get its act together in the hospitality department—it is shameful, really.

Americans are often disappointed to find central heating in hotels, meaning there is no control over the room temperature. If they like a cooler room at night, they will probably have to crank open the window, which, if facing a busy street, has its own noisy consequences.

Single travelers are sometimes shocked to discover their accommodations are little more than the size of a wardrobe closet. In America, most hotel rooms are alike, suites notwithstanding; but in Europe there is often a penalty for being single: one must pay more and get less.

Hotel bathrooms in Europe are sometimes ridiculously tiny, but there always seems to be space for a bidet, which perplexes many American men (what the hell is *that?*). Don't expect to find face cloths and body towels stocked in the bathrooms; in Italy, showers without curtains are common, and thin linen towels typically hang on the bathroom racks.

Breakfast Is Served

Based on our experience, breakfast is the most important meal of the day for Americans. Whenever possible, my company makes sure buffet breakfasts rather than continental breakfasts are included on its vacations, because if the day begins on a high note, it is likely to end on one. Europeans—with the exception of the British—do not generally eat omelets, fried or scrambled eggs, or breakfast meats in the morning. They typically have bread and cheese and cold cuts, such as thinly sliced ham or even liverwurst. Europeans also love yogurt for breakfast and strong coffee. Occasionally, they will treat themselves to a soft-boiled egg.

When Americans in Europe whine that their java tastes like tar, we tell them to add hot water to their cup. When they go "Ewwww!"

at the site of herring in dill sauce next to Knekkbroed (crisp bread), we remind them they are in Oslo. And whenever they complain about the greasiness of the eggs, bangers, and bacon in London, we suggest they dip into the pot of pork and beans next to the black pudding. "Ewwww!"

Understanding Europeans is the first step to enjoying a vacation on their turf. Despite what you've heard, the French don't hate Americans and don't go out of their way to be rude to us. In fact, the opposite is true, if one approaches them with a smile (this is true with any European, with the exception of the Belgians, who still have their noses out of joint for being used as doormats in both World Wars. Skip Belgium when touring Europe—Belgians are rude and there is nothing to see in Brussels but the Mannequin Piss, anyway). After Americans realize the French really do appreciate the role the U.S. played in saving their country in WWII (when the two Germanys united in 1989, former late night comic David Letterman reported that the French reacted by running backwards from that country, blowing air kisses), they lighten up and limit their globetrots to the price of Bordeaux wine.

Except for Republican presidents, the French have nothing against the United States (a sentiment shared by every country on earth. What is it with Republican presidents that makes the world itch?). It is *we* who have issues with the French. I once vented to a friend in Cannes my frustration with his lifestyle. "How can your country close shop from noon to 4 p.m.," I cried, upset that most businesses including banks and even gas stations shut down at midday on the French Riviera (the siesta is not practiced in Paris and other parts of France). "While the rest of the world is most productive during those hours, you all go home and eat, drink, and make love. Then, it's back to business for another three hours."

Dabbing the corners of his mouth with a folded napkin, my friend replied, "We think you Americans work too much." End of discussion. On reflection, though, he was probably right. Once again, I had fallen into the trap of wondering why another country could not be like the United States.

Not that Europeans are beyond reproach. Ever since *The Ugly American* was published in 1958, we have this fear of stepping out of line while on foreign soil. "I did not pack my usual assortment of Hawaiian shirts," senior travelers tell me, "because I didn't want to look like the Ugly American." Or "I refrained from mentioning to the waiter that dinner was cold—don't want to be construed as one of those Ugly Americans." Ironically, if you read the novel by Eugene Burdick and William Lederer, set in Southeast Asia, you will find no descriptions of the sort of image we now conjure up by the phrase "Ugly American." If anything, while abroad Americans are *too polite* when confronted by ill-mannered Swedes, Germans, Italians, Belgians, and the rest of the pack. One tends to forget that there are plenty of Ugly Europeans out there, too.

On a recent Italian cruise ship, I set out from Genoa on a three-week voyage with about 1,500 Europeans and 30 Americans. The lines at the buffet and at the Purser Desk were in utter chaos. It was the "first up, last served" as European seniors butted ahead of others, elbowing everyone in front of them. It was appalling and brought out the worst of me (I do not normally scold strangers but cut in front of me and I growl). Most disturbing was the ship's staff, all Italian, who interrupted serving those who were first in line to tend to those who had cut in. A crew member tried to explain away the boorish behavior of the guests by saying many European seniors were forced to scavenge during the years before and after World War II. To this day, their survival instinct is still evident.

Maybe, but that doesn't excuse rudeness. The fact is, as much as Americans complain to others behind closed doors and to their escorts and guides while on tour, they are often too polite in front of their foreign hosts and citizens. They tolerate more shenanigans abroad than they would in the U.S.

When you think about it, why *not* look American when exploring the streets of Toledo, Spain? Who wants to dress and act like a European? I say, be yourself and if you care to walk in shorts and a Hawaiian shirt, do so proudly. My late father used to don a western hat when he traveled to Europe, because he wore one at his home in Big Pine, California; and you know what? Europeans came up to him to shake his hand! Dad got it right—he was the same person away from his country as he was in it, and his lack of pretension (which, let's face it, is donning clothes other than what one wants to wear) made him more at ease as a traveler. Of course, there *are* areas of the planet—i.e., the Muslim world—where long pants should be worn, and shoulders be covered out of respect for custom and religion.

Europe isn't Disneyland, but Americans act like it is. "As long as I'm in Switzerland, I may as well go to Italy; and because Italy is below Germany, I want to go to Munich, as well. Isn't Salzburg, Austria, only two hours from that city? But wait—Switzerland also borders France, and I've always wanted to see Nice, which abuts

Monaco." In a single day at Disneyland, one can visit Fantasyland, Tomorrowland, Adventureland, and all the other "lands" before driving home, broke.

In Europe, though, one is talking about an entire continent, and crossing all those borders properly can take weeks plus *lots* of Euros, because most of the expressways are expensive toll roads. Unless one is taking a guided multi-country bus tour, a veritable Whitman's Sampler of nations as presented in the movie *If It's Tuesday, This Must Be Belgium*, travelers should factor in distance and limit their European "lands" to one or two. Don't forget that in addition to toll expenses, exorbitant insurance premiums and parking fees, the price of gasoline in the Old World is now about $8 a gallon.

Touring with a group by motor coach is the best way to see Europe for the 65+ generation, unless you are convinced you have the stamina of a teenager and can afford to risk your life behind a steering wheel. Who, older than 20 years of age, would want to challenge the continent's *autobahns, autostradas,* and *autoroutes*? The left lane on these expressways is strictly used for passing; if, in a forgetful moment, you find yourself inadvertently cruising that lane, a blast of horns and flashing high beams will awaken you to reality. Don't panic at what you see in the mirror: the radiator grille of that Mack truck isn't stuck to your rear bumper (yet); it just appears that way. There is a good five inches of space between you and that big rig--simply increase your speed to 120 MPH and get back into the right lane so that he can pass.

American seniors are sometimes attracted to the romance of rail travel in Europe, but at A.C.T. we try to talk them out of it. Like renting automobiles, taking trains, and purchasing Eurail Passes are best suited for the younger, backpack set (when senior citizens strap on backpacks, is it an attempt to recapture their lost youth? Someone should politely tell Aunt Mildred she looks ridiculous). Kids have no problem jumping off and on trains. Many older Americans can't decipher rail schedules posted in noisy, drafty train stations, which are often infested with pickpockets and gypsies.

I recall two women, both in their late seventies, who ignored our warnings about train travel in Europe and insisted A.C.T. arrange for them to "hop" aboard trains, starting in Marseilles, France, on a journey that ended in Barcelona, Spain.

"You failed to tell us there would be no porters!" they complained upon their return to the U.S. "We couldn't lift our bags onto the cars. And we missed our connection in Narbonne—you only gave us an hour there to figure out where to go." *No porters?* Nonsense. *Only* 60 minutes at a town train station to make a connection. Seems a reasonable amount of time to go from one platform to another. Once again it was our fault, and the search continues to find even *one* traveler who will take responsibility for his or her decisions.

Travel by rail in Europe can be enjoyable, however, especially if the rides are day journeys and are part of an organized tour handled by professionals. Three train itineraries I especially enjoy including are following the Rhine River, going through the Brenner Pass (from Austria to Italy), and traversing the Alps in Switzerland. The coastal routes on the French Riviera (to Monaco) and Spain's Costa del Sol are also beautiful. Day-tripping by rail is somewhat easy to arrange and is recommended if one has the time. It is not to be confused with travel in Europe *solely* by train, which for said reasons is often arduous.

Finally, a word about the speedy Eurostar trains traveling through the Chunnel, and the sleek TVG rail cars that connect Paris to major cites in France. Their routes are functional, not particularly scenic. Passengers arrive in a timely manner, but travel is so fast that Americans often feel disappointed in the actual ride. Oh, and taking the pricey, fabled Orient Express is not as lavish as Agatha Christie would have you believe. The communal bathrooms are down the hall, the least expensive sleeper cars are bunk-style, and after departing Paris, the classic train travels 48 hours non-stop to Venice. Like a never-ending international flight, the thing just keeps going (Orient *Express*—get it?) until it chokes to a stop at the same dank stations used by public trains. A.C.T. has never offered rail journeys on the Orient Express for that reason.

It is only logical to suggest Great Britain as the first country to visit on a maiden voyage to Europe (the English speak our language, after all), but that doesn't stop some Americans from getting their feet wet with countries like Serbia, Ukraine, and Russia. Bad choices, because the negative impressions these backward countries can leave may be a turnoff to future vacations to Western Europe. Not only is the infrastructure in eastern European countries bad, but the entire region is also not particularly "fun." Poland was, as everyone knows, devastated in World War II and is still recovering; the death camps there are almost too much to bear. The Baltic countries like Latvia and Estonia offer little to visitors (you know a tourist board is desperate when it promotes folkloric shows as "must-sees"), and there's not a lot to rave about touring Romania, Bratislava, and Hungary (graffiti-filled Budapest notwithstanding). Only Prague, capital of the Czech Republic, captures the charm of Old Europe, and as a result the city is usually swamped with tourists, all looking for the St. Charles Bridge.

Russia's cultural hub, St. Petersburg, is a favorite of Americans, As is Moscow, the country's political capital, transformed in recent years to something resembling Gotham City (it's interesting how an influx of money can affect a city); but one always feels relief when departing the former Soviet Union. Let's just say there are not many smiling faces there. As one traveler observed, swatting the air as if to wipe her hands clean of the entire country, "After climbing those stairs at the Hermitage and Pushkin, I need Russia like it needs a revolution."

CHATTING WITH MOSCOW GUIDES IN RED SQUARE,
SOVIET UNION (PRE-RUSSIA)

Social Realism—that self-same, dreary architectural style of buildings pervasive in former Soviet bloc nations—adds to the depressive nature of Eastern Europe. I suppose one *could* argue that prices are cheaper east of Austria, but other than that, why would anyone care to vacation in Bulgaria?

Cruising the Danube River from Vienna to Bucharest or to Constanta on the Black Sea is the best way to tour Eastern Europe, as the boat typically stops in six or seven countries. In addition to unpacking once, passengers return to the safety and comfort of their floating hotel after getting their heels scuffed in muddy Balkan wanna-be tourist towns. And as they sail merrily away from ports like Vidin, Mohac, and Giurgiu, Americans gripe at being served yet another cabbage dinner salad, failing to realize that bibs of iceberg lettuce do not exist in Dracula countries.

Back to the future, which is to say, Western Europe. It's sort of pathetic when, on the sidewalks of London, one sees the words "Look right" and "Look left" painted on street corners, reminding Americans that--in their jargon—the English drive cars "on the wrong side of the road." Apparently, quite a few Yanks have met their fate jaywalking, forgetting where they were, and London officials felt they had to do something. Reminding tourists to look before crossing streets is just one example of how polite the English are. More than anywhere else in Europe, Great Britain—including Northern Ireland--rolls out the red carpet for Americans. Northern Ireland is a fascinating country whose revitalized capital, Belfast, is one of the hippest places to party these days, despite its religious foibles (most people don't know it, but there is still an enormous wall dividing Belfast: Catholics on one side, Protestants on the other. Move over, Berlin of the past).

When Americans return complaining about the food in the British Isles, I ask if they went to a carvery while there. Inevitably, the answer is no, only Indian restaurants and pubs were affordable, the latter establishment offering diners boiled organs and steak and kidney pies. Carveries are quiet, quintessentially English eating establishments that should not be missed. Enormous metal serving carts are rolled to the table and, when the hood is pulled back, patrons are presented a selection of simmering meats--English roast beef, pork loin, and spring lamb--that are carved before their eyes. There is also an assortment of fowl to choose from (try the duck and guinea hens). Yorkshire pudding, roast potatoes, and green vegetables round out the unforgettable meal.

So why have most Americans never heard of carveries? Because they're not mentioned in *Frommer's Guides* or books by Fodor, two popular travel publications whose primary function is to advise readers on how to see Europe on the cheap. The same is true with the darling of PBS, Rick Steves, who touts the virtues of backpacking in Europe and staying in 2-star hotels or hostels where bathrooms are located down the hall. As a result, gullible seniors seek out "socca," a yucky, poor man's version of pizza sold in the seedy Old Town section of Nice and buy "polska" sausages from street vendors in Copenhagen instead of experiencing a real Danish smorgasbord. As one gets older, cheap meals and plastic souvenirs of Big Ben and the Eiffel Tower need to be replaced with breaking bread in intimate restaurants with friends or spouses. Instead, because of youth-oriented guidebooks or on the advice of a rich television entrepreneur disguised as Everyman with a Backpack, seniors attempt to eat and live, in their minds, like the locals. The fact is, it is very doubtful that Messrs. Frommer, Fodor, or Steves—let alone the majority of local yokels--would want to even be seen eating at such outlets. Still, these travel experts inspire their devotees to do just that and—like sheep—Americans, armed with maps, notes, and backpacks—take their advice, missing in the process the chance to sample cuisine really worth writing home about.

This means Americans are advised to occasionally skip a meal that is included on a tour's itinerary. Recently, on an autumn Danube River cruise through Hungary, Lalo Alvarez (vice-president of A.C.T.) and I decided to pass up an included shore tour of the small town of Pecs (no great loss there, we figured), in favor of having lunch somewhere off the boat in a local setting. We followed the river for about a half mile and stumbled upon a local, bucolic restaurant and ordered homemade goulash, a specialty of the country, and a bottle of red Hungarian wine. The day was cold, and the delicious stew—served hot with freshly baked bread—was unforgettable.

"Where were *you?*" groused others in our group, after they returned to the boat from their guided excursion. "As our bus drove away, we saw you two wandering the countryside."

I answered honestly, and my mistake was describing our lunch.

"Why didn't you tell *us?*" one man asked in anger. "Did you ever think maybe *we* would have liked to do that, instead of visiting a town no one has heard of?"

I was too polite to ask why the thought of dining locally, far from the madding crowd, had not occurred to him, because so many interesting things can happen when one leaves the pack. It is amazing how people can resent it when they see others doing just that.

His wife eventually rescued me, rhetorically asking him why he would want to pay for a lunch when it was included on the boat.

"You're right," he said, and off they went to dive into their cabbage salads.

Take this advice: Even if it's not part of the program, go to tapas bars in Spain and, like a native, try the little dishes of appetizers offered there. In Sweden, join the locals during the Crayfish Festival and suck the juices from the little buggers. In Germany, sample the many types of wursts (and don't overlook the *Leberkase*). Go to a Dublin pub not included in your program, sit with the locals and drink a Guinness with them even if you don't like dark beer. In Austria, order the frothy *Salzburgerknockerel,* a dessert in Salzburg sweeter than Maria Von Trapp; and in Vienna, sip the finest coffee in the world at the Sacher Hotel with a serving of Sacher Torte cake. Discover how these experiences really make the best souvenirs and *forget about the cost!* Do research about specialty foods and drinks and dining establishments before you leave home, and your vacation will be twice as fulfilling.

*I often tell people that getting lost in a city—literally—is something not to dread, but to embrace. When that happens, one usually seeks help to find his way back, which means communicating with foreigners. That can lead to new friendships and maybe even a free ride back to the hotel. Getting lost can take you through byways and neighborhoods you otherwise would not have seen, and the stories on how you "survived" the ordeal are more enjoyable to your neighbors than how all went right on your vacation.

For that reason, on cruise ships I suggest skipping the pricey shore excursions and hailing a taxi instead. Cab drivers love to share with you their city or countryside, and they know where to take you for the best local cuisine. In addition, you can interact with them—i.e., ask questions and respond to their commentary, all for usually a fraction of what the ship charges.

Travel through Europe from its southernmost point to its most northern, and what a range of *behavior* you will witness! The entire trip by automobile is now possible, thanks to the Oresund Bridge connecting Sweden to Denmark. Imagine driving from Athens to Lapland without ever taking a ferry. From the land of Zorba, you would drive north through the Adriatic countries, former Yugoslavia on one side of the sea and Italy on the other. Interesting how those countries are similar—although both have reputations for hot-headed people (Italy has had something like 50 governments since World War II, and the Balkan nations have only recently stopped fighting), they are also culturally rich. Continuing through the Alps, leaving the Latin countries behind, one enters cool-headed Germany: Munich in southern Bavaria hosts far more festivals and is—what, friendlier? —than northern German cities like Bremen and Lubeck (the best read capturing the difference between Germanic and Latin peoples is Thomas Mann's brilliant novella, *Death in Venice*). By the time you get to Oslo, Europe's most northern capital, it's all logic with little heart, let alone humor, the exact opposite of where you had started.

**To see if Europe could laugh at itself, Czech artist David Cerny painted a ferocious parody of stereotypes of the EU countries in 2009, a canvas depicting his vision of European harmony. Cerny's "Poland is represented by catholic monks posed as the Marines at Iwo Jima, but they are raising the rainbow flag of the gay rights movement; Luxembourg is a lump of gold with a 'for sale' sign; Germany is a series of highways (resembling a swastika), and all of France is on strike.

Romania is one big Dracula theme park, and Bulgaria is portrayed as a series of squat toilets." Said European countries were *not* amused, and some have summoned Czech ambassadors to their capitals to explain the artist's humor.

Scandinavia is an entity unto itself. I once spent July and August in southern Sweden's *Skane* region and attended a Summer Solstice party. Scandinavians celebrate the year's longest day, probably because they get so little sun. At the structured event, they make elaborate toasts with gooseberry wine and skip around maypoles. I commented to a partygoer that few tourists there seemed to be in his country.

"Sweden is for Swedes," he sniffed, without smiling.

On another occasion, at a formal dinner in Karlskrona, I was asked if I was proud to be American.

"Yes, of course," I answered. "Why do you ask?"

"Because from what we see on television, I can't understand why anyone would be proud." I made up my mind then and there not to give him one of the Kennedy half dollars that I had packed to hand out as souvenirs. The news is so slanted to the left in socialist Scandinavia, there was no use responding.

So, other than taking a cruise ship to these expensive lands (the cheapest way to go), is it worthwhile driving to Denmark, Sweden, Norway, and Finland?

No.

Sure, Scandinavia probably has the best soft ice cream in the world (less air and more butter fat), and those fjords in Norway are indeed scenic. But so are the ones in Alaska, Chile, and New Zealand at half the cost.

Shrimp, served on an open-face sandwich in Denmark, is delicious, but for the same price I could buy 14 shrimp cocktails in downtown Las Vegas. And the blue-eyed blonde babes who used to attract horny Japanese and Americans tourists are rare these days, ever since Romanians, Poles, Armenians, and refugees from African and Muslim countries impregnated the Nordic lassies while in search of work.

It's not just about money and food, though; there's a weirdness about Scandinavia, perhaps because the countries are far removed from the rest of Europe. In the heart of Oslo's Vigeland Park, for example, on a public expanse of lawn and shade trees, stand enormous anatomically correct statues of naked, contorted humans. The dozens of figures lead to a 30 foot-high, dildo-shaped tower of sculpted nudes climbing over each other--the perfect setting for a family picnic.

"WATCH YOUR HAND BUDDY!" CRUISING THE FJORDS OF NORWAY

In Sweden, people wear wooden clogs and dash outside their offices during summer every chance they get to soak up sunshine. Sometimes, the women remove their blouses and sit topless before returning to work. No one cares. Swedes eat dried Baltic eels and suck salt licorice, adhere to ridiculous laws (i.e., agreeing to use only government approved colors for their houses), and provide the unemployed not only free homes, but summer country houses as well. Plus, they still dance around maypoles....

Denmark, especially Copenhagen, a big university capital, can be energetic, but the Danes value booze more than border protection. The country's liberal socialism has allowed thousands of not-so-complacent Muslim refugees to "take over." Everyone remembers the flap over cartoons depicting Mohammed, published in the largest newspaper there. Riots, boycotts of Danish goods, and threats against journalists and government officials followed. That sort of took the fun out of Wonderful, Wonderful Copenhagen, where Tivoli Gardens, Hans Christian Andersen, and the Little Mermaid once delighted tourists.

Outside of the tiny capital, Helsinki, what is there to see in Finland? In fact, what is there to see in Helsinki? It's a piss stop on the way to St. Petersburg, Russia.

I say, Scandinavia is for Scandinavians.

So where in Europe do Americans whine the least? Probably in Italy if the tour operator is on his toes. The country offers it all—picturesque lakes, breathtaking mountains and hillside postcard towns, pristine coastlines with glamorous resorts, Sicily and Capri, the world's favorite cuisine, and (oh yeah) glorious history, art, and that place where the Pope lives, Vatican City. No one seems to tire of Italy's Golden Triangle—Rome, Florence, and Venice.

France and England come in second and third, and then, probably, Spain and Ireland. What surprises me is the lack of interest Americans have in Germany, a reunited country that is also steeped in history, most recently of the military kind (maybe that accounts for the disinterest).   There are great museums in Germany, but few Americans know about them.

***An "organized tour" of Italy is an oxymoron, because practically everything in the country is *tutti fruity*. Italy is either on strike, payoffs are demanded, or it's an obscure religious feast day and everything is closed. Americans love the Land of Pasta, but from a professional point of view, Italy is one of the world's toughest nuts to crack and requires vigilance to pull off a successful trip.

The Netherlands, Portugal, Switzerland, and Scotland, and other has a distinct heritage, but offer nothing special, unless your family is from there or you like (respectively) tulips, Mateus wine, yodeling, and bagpipes. Amsterdam, capital of Holland, is a favorite of young people and druggies, as well as salacious men who have no idea where Anne Frank's historic home is but do know where to find every house of ill repute in the Red-Light District.   Disappointment often is the reaction of people first exposed to Portugal's Algarve coast, and I have yet to meet anyone who is crazy about Lisbon (too hilly and not pedestrian-friendly like Barcelona and Prague).

Switzerland, if mountains are your thing, is situated, as everyone knows, in the middle of Europe. Most American seniors, not crazy about endless tunnels and high altitudes, prefer to skirt around the country by either following the French Riviera or going through Germany's Brenner Pass. Switzerland is just too expensive, and who--outside of those visitors to Lucerne, Geneva, or Zurich--has ever heard of Bucherer watches?

Lest you think these are the words of a tired and jaded traveler whose negativity is about to consume him, allow me to go on record to say that some of my best travel memories have occurred in Europe. In no particular order:

--I remember beaming with pride at my grandfather, who actually yodeled *in harmony* with a professional Swiss entertainer on stage at the Stadtkeller Restaurant in Lucerne.

--I remember at 21 years old viewing the English Channel from the chalky cliffs of Dover, after hiking up there with my brother, thinking of World Wars, Matthew Arnold, bluebirds, and the famous scene from *King Lear.*

--I remember visiting the great museums in Europe, as millions before me have done, and admiring the masterpieces. J. Paul Getty, who visited art galleries after graduating from Oxford College, was so moved by works in the Prado, Louvre, and Hermitage, that he started assembling his own European art collection, which is now exhibited at the Getty Center in Brentwood and Malibu.

--I remember furtively being taken to a secluded garage in Berchtesgaden, Germany, to examine the original carved sign that had hung over the train station in 1941, depicting an eagle clutching an enormous swastika in its talons. I was asked in whispers if I was interested in buying it. (The answer was "no").

--I remember chasing gypsies in one train door and out another, at the much-heralded underground Moscow subway station after they stole Lalo's wallet. It was eventually recovered, intact.

--I remember losing forever my passport and camera to thieves in Rome, just after warning my group of travelers to "beware of pickpockets."

--I remember dancing in a Spanish discotheque until dawn, and marveling at the number of local senior citizens who were up that late and who closed the place with me. Some were in their 80's!

--I remember attending *wonderful* private music recitals in Eastern Europe, from classical opera in Romania to Chopin piano concertos in Poland.

--I remember as a teacher, taking my high school students to a Viennese disco and watching them dance with native kids to music by Michael Jackson, only to have them clear the floors in amazement when their foreign peers whirled and twirled in perfect step to the next tune, Johann Strauss' *Waltz of Blue Danube.*

--I remember being asked by an East German family to help them escape their country, and by a Russian boy to escape his. I succeeded in aiding the latter.

--I remember sailing with my friend in his private boat off of Antibes in the South of France, almost tipping over, and later getting tipsy on champagne at his family's condo in St. Tropez

--I remember running into Princess Stephanie outside the Cathedral in Monaco where her parents are buried.

--I remember being handed the baton in Munich during Oktoberfest and leading the orchestra inside the event's largest tent, with thousands of Germans swaying to the music below me.

--I remember some of the finest meals being in Europe, from Belgian fries (served with mustard mayonnaise) to pesto tortellini in Italy and virtually every dish in France, where it is impossible to get a bad meal. Boy, do I remember.

STEVE'S FAVORITE REGION IN EUROPE, THE FRENCH RIVIERA (ANTIBES)

The recollection that stays with me the most, however, the one that epitomizes Europe, happened on the island of Capri, Italy, in 1995. The lure of Capri with its citrus trees, azure waters, and breathtaking landscapes has attracted tourists for over 2,000 years. The island, just off the Amalfi coast and a 20-minute ferry ride from Naples, has been the favorite escape of jetsetters and movie stars, because the weather is almost always pleasant and no one bothers anyone in Capri Town, where everybody dines outdoors without fear of being accosted by paparazzi or common folk. Capri Town during summer is one big outdoor festival.

I decided to take a walk from all the action and follow the sound of instrumental music that was playing across a verdant park. I stopped at an area overlooking lush Italian gardens. Below me was a wedding reception, complete with a four-piece band, and the bride and groom were dancing to *The Merry Widow Waltz*, surrounded by admiring guests who had formed a ring around them. The bride in her white wedding dress was stunningly beautiful, and her young husband—clad in a tuxedo with long coat tails—conjured up the stereotypical handsome Italian male. A light breeze from the Mediterranean Sea kept the guests comfortable and bathed the area with the scent of lemon blossoms. Nearby, children played with wedding balloons, and across the Bay of Naples, Mount Vesuvius slept peacefully on the mainland.

This was uniquely a European moment, because in the United States, the wedding reception typically would have been staged indoors, accompanied by rock and roll music. The dancing couple below me, coddled by the warm glow of the Mediterranean Sea, had as their wedding backdrop the actual remains of the villa where Tiberius, Emperor of the Roman Empire, received word that Christ had been crucified.

"A powerful overflow of spontaneous feelings" is how William Wordsworth defined poetry. On that sunny afternoon in Capri, the same might have been said about Europe.

ASIA

"My, this city has a big China Town!"

—UTTERED BY A DISORIENTED SENIOR DURING AN
A.C.T. TOUR OF HONG KONG

Ah, the effect Asia has on Americans. Maybe the jet lag from the long flight has something to do with it, or the sight of fried grasshoppers mixed into their salads. It could be the exotic modes of Far East transportation, from elephants in Jaipur to *tuk-tuks* in Bangkok and pedicabs in Beijing. East is East, after all, and West is West; there is nothing like a visit to Cambodia, Myanmar, or Laos to make one realize he's not in Kansas anymore. But, really, isn't that what foreign travel *should* be about, exposure to DIFFERENT cultures, foods, religions, and history?

You'd think so, but many U.S. citizens feel otherwise. Outside of Pearl Harbor, few Americans are interested in or can even relate to Asian history. As far as religion is concerned, the tenets of Buddhism, Hinduism, Taoism, and Confucianism become blurred, leaving lots of westerners scratching their heads. Grandpa and Grandma reincarnated as wandering cows in New Delhi? Sure, I can buy that. Praying to the Jade Buddha for good fortune, or lighting incense in honor of Ganesh, the multi-armed elephant? It's a stretch, but on the other hand, we Yanks *do* have our lucky rabbit feet and shamrocks. Still, when a guide in Bali, Indonesia once pointed out an ornate Hindu pagoda in the middle of Lake Batur and said (with a straight face) that it served as God's washroom, I felt compelled to ask—after hearing similar nonsense for eight straight days—if he actually believed that fantasy.

"Why, yes," he answered matter of factly. "And I suppose *you* think Jesus walked on water." *Touche!*

VOID OF TOURISTS AT THE GREAT WALL. CHINA

People sort of know what Ireland is like before their first trip to the Emerald Isle, but China always manages to surprise newcomers. In Beijing, millions of bicycles have been replaced by luxury cars, and western eateries like Tony Roma's, Ruth's Chris Steakhouse, Starbucks, and Pizza Hut abound. Western architecture is everywhere, and modern hotels of every class—all built within the last 50 years—proliferate the country. Americans who were admonished by their parents to "eat all you've been served—think of the starving people in China" are sometimes aghast at the number of obese people populating the People's Republic, especially children, who have been pampered by their doting, newly affluent parents. When the government mandated only one child per family, you could bet that when China's economy exploded, so did the waist size of the spoiled little dears.

Before the 2008 Olympics, a popular perception was that China was a poor nation. After a dose of reality, American tourists usually returned pleasantly surprised by the modernity of the country. Other than the usual moans about walking and climbing too many steps (including ascending muddy banks of the Yangtze River and at the Great Wall) and gagging at the native cuisine ("This slop doesn't compare to The Golden Dragon Restaurant in our town--where's the soy sauce?"), folks from Pretoria are overwhelmed by the enormity of China. As one awestruck tourist told me in Shanghai, "To think that all of *this* is going on while I sleep in America!"

My impression of China is mixed. While some sites are indeed impressive (seeing the Great Wall for the first time—like viewing the Pyramids—reduces us to giddy kids at Christmas time), I am inclined to believe that if the communist government decreed Americans should be spit upon in the streets, the Chinese people would do so without hesitation. There are so *many* of them that at times, one feels he is surrounded by army ants. Displayed in Beijing's Tianamen Square is the famous portrait of Mao Zedong, which begs one to question why it still hangs. After all, between his failed programs, The Great Leap Forward and The Cultural Revolution, Chairman Mao was responsible for the deaths of some 50 million Chinese, either by starvation or murder. Millions of others were sent to re-education camps and subjected to hard labor. In the 21st century, why do the Chinese idolize their late, not-so-great leader? Have they forgotten or—worst yet--*forgiven* the devastation he caused?

Food served in China is truly not as tasty as that found in the U.S. It is greasy and M.S.G. is used in practically all of the dishes. Fish is served whole, with head and tail still intact, so turned-off Americans often make white rice the meal of the day. Part of the problem is the window dressing seen outside street restaurants and wet markets, things like hanging plucked ducks appearing as though they had been strangled, and severed pigs' heads on chopping blocks. Then there are the jars of pickled snakes and brown "1,000-year-old" duck eggs.

*Someone should write a book on how America has improved international cuisine. The meals in China, Italy, Mexico, Spain, and scores of other countries are less tasty than those prepared in the U.S., where dishes are lighter, better spiced, and often fresher than in their native lands. It is still a challenge to find wurst, schnitzel, and beer as good as in Germany, though; and cuisine in France is the finest in the world.

As tourists, we travel to foreign countries to experience things different from our own culture, but--being American--we often are repulsed by those differences. It works both ways, of course; bring out a piece of cheese to snack on, and Chinese typically react like Dracula confronting the crucifix. They wince and turn away, because 1) the smell of cheese offends them and 2) dairy products, in general, are repugnant to them. Except at tourist hotels, don't look for milk, butter, cheeses, or even ice cream in the People's Republic.

Things that bother western tourists often don't upset the Chinese, like cleanliness. We have witnessed maids aboard Yangtze riverboats using the same rags on drinking glasses that moments before had wiped toilet bowls clean. Loudly clearing one's throat and hurling on public sidewalks is common among the Chinese. Magnificent four and five- star hotels, gorgeously furnished, are often marred by carpets that are woefully stained. Management cannot understand why this minor imperfection would perturb Americans, or why the phrase "Just one moment please" uttered by hotel staff every time a question is asked bugs the hell out of us. Hospitality has a long way to go in China before the country catches up with the rest of the world.

"HAVE I MET YOU BEFORE? YOUR FACE RINGS FAMILIAR."
CHIANG RAI, THAILAND

Not so in Thailand, formerly Siam, where service and cleanliness in even two-star hotels are taken seriously. What an incredible, diversified country the "Land of Smiles" is! From elephant treks in Chiang Mai and shopping sprees in sexy Bangkok, and from the pristine beaches of Phuket to the exotic hill tribes in Chiang Rai, Thailand is one big amusement park. Rivers teeming with history and culture, like the mighty Chao Phraya dividing the capital and the infamous Kwai River a hundred miles south, offer tourists the chance to board boats for exotic cruises. Colorful floating markets, three-wheeled *tuk-tuks*, and satays smothered in peanut sauce are among the wonderful memories' visitors bring back.

**Pizza parlors, of course, are the exception in China, as well as hamburger franchises, which offer cheeseburgers. Both venues cater primarily to westerners, who crave anything cheesy after digesting food made in woks for days on end.

The southeast Asian country is enthralling to everyone except those afflicted with globetrots. In Thailand, whining Americans complain of humidity and heat, pollution, native music, and even Patpong, Bangkok's red-light district (I always wonder how these contemptuous souls find their way to that lurid area; it's not one that a person just stumbles across). Miserable travelers cry about having to remove their shoes before entering Buddhist temples, and they make no attempt to learn the gentle customs of the land, like the "wai" (forming hands into a steeple and bowing when being introduced), or simple Thai words. Rather than spend $4 on a fun, open-air *tuk-tuk* taxi used by the locals, globetrotters summon to their hotels air-conditioned cabs, and then complain about the thirty bucks they have to shell out to drive across town.

Outside of Japan and Singapore—two countries whose modernity is no surprise to western visitors (hence a resistance among many Americans to go there)—Asia can be quite an eye-opener. Take Vietnam, for example. Bicycles and motor scooters are still the way most people get around in the country. Fine hotels are being built there, and the country boasts a number of World Heritage sites, such as dreamy Halong Bay in the North. Vietnam's handicrafts are different from other Asian nations—things like carved marble from the DaNang area, and lacquered pictures in the South inlaid with eggshells. Most surprising to many Americans is the friendliness of the people. They ostensibly harbor no ill feelings toward U.S. citizens who—along with armies of both North and South Vietnam—ravished the nation in the 60's and 70's. "We Vietnamese understand," I was told by our elderly guide in Ho Chi Minh City, formerly Saigon, "that America's intentions were noble."

The Vietnam War is the proverbial elephant in the room that no credible guide there can ignore. Thousands of ponds still pockmark the land, formed by bomb craters. China Beach is eerily deserted now, and the foggy shoreline is haunted by ghosts of U.S. servicemen. The underground tunnels and spider traps used by the Viet Cong, almost invisible to the eye, near Ho Chi Minh City are a testament to the horrors of guerilla warfare that our soldiers experienced. American infantrymen didn't have a chance.

This is travel at its enlightening best. While sometimes somber, Vietnam is breathtakingly vibrant and beautiful. It is one of those countries that leaves Americans sighing and crying.

Other Asian nations that seek American tourists may not be worth the expense and hassle of visiting. What does Malaysia offer, really? Hot and humid, the peninsula has three major attractions: the capital of Kuala Lumpur, Penang Island, and Langkawi Islands. The first is crowded and smoggy, the second is colorless, and Langkawi, promoted by the country as a "must see" collection of pristine islands, is surrounded by muddy waters that are too creepy to dip into.

Indonesia has two main attractions, Bali and—in Central Java near Yogyakarta—the mountainous Temple of Borobudur. Bali has lost its allure to many following two terrorist bombing attacks in the 1990's, and the "breathtaking" beaches of Kuta and Nusa Dua are disappointments when compared to other famous strands of the world. Jakarta, on the island of Java, is the capital of Indonesia and is a teeming snake pit of Islamic mischief. No surprise that State Department travel warnings are permanently posted about going there. Having said that, the island's Borobudur Temple—the largest Buddhist temple in the world—is worthy of a visit, as is the Hindu Prambanan Temple nearby. It is sad that in this era of Islamic terrorism, one can risk his life traveling to Jakarta. Therefore, we say skip Yogyakarta (which means, ironically, "prosperity without war") and Borobudur in favor of the temples of Angkor Wat, Cambodia.

The four or five complexes of lost-then-found 12th century temples surrounding Angkor Wat outside the town of Siem Reap are truly impressive but climbing the narrow steps to the top is a cakewalk compared to descending them. The steps were purposely designed to be narrow to keep feet pointed away from the peak (it is not polite in the Hindu religion to aim toes at people or at religious deities), and without a handrail the steep decline can be dangerous and harrowing.

TOMB RAIDER LALO ALVAREZ EXPLORES
ANGKOR WAT, CAMBODIA

Other than Angkor Wat, poverty and landmines are the only notable "attractions" of Cambodia. For better or worse, visiting the Killing Fields is a chilling experience. Laos, south of Cambodia, is a struggling country still healing from the Vietnam War and is not a particularly popular destination. For some, being immersed in poor living conditions earns the recognition of being a "traveler" rather than a "tourist." But unless there is something significant to see in such a community, *why go there?* We know poverty exists without having to experience it.

Too bad more Americans don't travel to the Southeast Asian country of Myanmar, formerly known as Burma. This is the way Thailand looked 100 years ago, but the natural beauty of Burma is more exquisite. Bordered by China, Thailand, Laos, and Malaysia, Myanmar is all over the board in terms of geography: tropical jungles, winding rivers, pristine lakes, and the towering Himalayas. With the exception of the cruel junta military leaders, sweeter people you will never meet. Devout Buddhists, Burmese welcome westerners and especially Americans, who often mistakenly believe there is a Cuba-type ban from entering the country. There is not, and the question arises whether the U.S. government's discouraging of travel to Myanmar hasn't backfired and hurt the gentle populace, who badly need tourist dollars. The perception that to travel there is dangerous may actually help the thuggish government, which is probably happy to keep western influence out of the country. The few tourists who do decide to visit Myanmar return amazed at the enormous golden Schwedagon Pagoda in Yangon, and at the fishermen on Lake Inle who row boats with oars strapped to their legs, and at the thousands of temples and stupas dotting the Irrawaddy River valley in Bagen. Say "Road to Mandalay" and all kinds of romantic, exotic fantasies come to mind. I'm happy to report that, in reality those images are all true.

CAN YOU SPOT THE TOURIST?
LALO IN MYANMAR (FORMERLY BURMA)

It has always puzzled me why India is not considered the world's eighth continent, rather than a subcontinent. Larger than Australia, almost the size of South America, India is not really a part of Asia, but is lumped in with other countries there because of its geographical location. It is in reality thousands of miles away from Southeast Asia, and the differences between New Delhi and Beijing are about as apparent as Las Vegas and Kansas City.

Most American visitors to India travel experience what is known as The Golden Triangle, starting in New Delhi, the country's capital, and continuing through the ancient trading city of Jaipur before reaching Agra, home of the Taj Mahal. Few continue to Khajuraho, where the Temples of Kama Sutra are located, and to the holy city of Varanasi on the Ganges River. Those who travel further south, to the Muslim states, are fewer still. Whatever region in the country Americans tour, the reaction is usually the same: they either love India or hate it.

One Globetrotter wrote after his vacation how "filthy everything was—roads with potholes, stinky street scenes, crowded train cars, and even beggars."

Do you think?

"How could you take us to such a country!" he chided. Again, blame your travel agent for booking a destination you opted to visit.

The pampered man inflicted with globetrots did not appreciate what many who visit India embrace: exotic women wearing colorful saris, roadside elephants, and camels (talk about sights!), and wonderful curry-flavored foods. He apparently did not notice the smiles on the faces of the dirty street kids, nor was he interested in the love story surrounding the Taj Mahal. Perhaps expecting Eiffel Towers and romantic gondolas, the man got instead Fort Jaipur and, at dawn in Varanasi, a longboat ride past funeral pyres on the Ganges River. It is amazing the number of people who apparently do not read the itinerary before signing up for a trip.

A.C.T. GROUP AT THE TAJ MAHAL, INDIA

I love India; as in the case with China, it is one of those great nations *on the move*. With each visit, improvements are noticeable in all aspects, from economics and infrastructure to lodgings (like other Third World countries, India boasts a variety of excellent 5-star hotels, accommodations that are essential for the American visitor). The shopping is great, the people are friendly, and the culture, steeped in Hinduism (yes, wandering cows really do have the right of way), is a way of life. Tours to India are often complemented with a visit to Kathmandu, Nepal. Once again, the effect a visit to both India and Nepal can produce is appreciation for America's lifestyle and blessings.

The same can be said about a trip to Mongolia and Tibet. Oh lord, why didn't the ground operator there forewarn us that outside of Mongolia's capital, Ulaanbaatar, there are no toilets? Crossing the Gobi Desert in a convoy of vans, we finally stopped in the middle of nowhere for a comfort break. One of our female sophisticates painfully exited the Soviet-made vehicle and, rubbing her back, asked our guide, "Where is the powder room?" She was directed to a nearby bush.

Lack of facilities extended to our accommodations in yurts, a.k.a. as "gers," which are nothing more than round tents. Don't look for hotels outside Ulaanbaatar; Mongolian horsemen and camel herders live in yurts, which dot the desert landscape and can easily be dismantled and moved. Candles provide lighting inside of them, as electricity is practically non-existent beyond the cities. Sound like a fun vacation? Only if you're Genghis Khan or are a camping buff.

"I'LL RACE YOU UP THE STAIRS! POTOLA PALACE, TIBET

Lhasa in Tibet, at 9,842 feet in elevation, is the highest capital in the world, or at least it is the highest in an autonomous region. China lays claim to the Himalayan "Roof of the World" and—as is the case with Taiwan --there is much controversy over territorial rights. In any case, sitting on a hilltop in Lhasa is the Potala Palace, the Dalai Lama's former winter home, as well as Jokhang Temple, the spiritual center of Tibet and a pilgrimage site, containing a golden statue of Buddha. Tibet, whose population is 91% Buddhist, shares Mt. Everest with Nepal, 81% Hindu. Either country makes an interesting three-day stop after touring China, India, or Mongolia.

Sometimes the best souvenirs on a vacation are conversations one has with native citizens. From my travel journal to Tibet, the following piece is aptly titled "If Only":

Today was a bright, cloudless day in the former Kingdom of Tibet, high in the Himalayas. While taking a tour of the capital, Lhasa, I stopped to catch my breath at the imposing Potala Palace, home of the exiled Dalai Lama. Our guide continued ascending endless steps leading into the Palace with the group, but I lingered in a shady courtyard and noticed a pair of Chinese teenage girls giggling and taking photos with their smart phones. I asked them where they were from, and they answered Shanghai.

"Why Lhasa?" I asked. "Why did you choose to come here?"

In perfect English, one smiled and, pointing above, sighed, "We both wanted to see what a blue sky looked like. If only we could live here!" Having traveled to industrial Shanghai on the East China Sea in the past, I can attest to the sprawling city's polluted air. It is true—I have never experienced a smog-free day in Shanghai, and as thin as the atmosphere is here in Tibet, the sky's color is undeniably azure.

Later in afternoon at our hotel, a bellman delivered a shirt I had ordered and at my invitation, stayed a few moments to chat. Mark Qie, as he was named, lamented that the Chinese government now ruled Tibet and natives like himself were seldom granted permission to travel outside the mountainous country.

"Where would go, if you could?" I asked him.

"Shanghai," he answered, "to experience the sea. If only I were allowed to visit Shanghai...."

AFRICA AND THE MIDEAST

"So where do the tigers hang out?"

- QUERY POSED TO OUR GAME SPOTTER IN KRUGER PARK, SOUTH AFRICA

Think of Africa, and what pops into your head? Wild animals, of course, which would *not* include tigers, as they are indigenous to India and certain regions of Asia. Violence, famine, and more than one thug leader also come to mind when mentioning the Dark Continent. Apartheid, the Serengeti, the Great Migration, Victoria Falls, A.I.D.S., the earliest man—these, too, are images that one conjures up in that single word, "Africa." Throw in Hemingway and Mt. Kilimanjaro and we're done.

But it's mostly the exciting game drives that Americans think of, often forgetting that the ancient Pyramids, historic Carthage, and trendy Red Sea resorts are also part of Africa. Even crossing the Strait of Gibraltar from Europe for a half day of shopping in Tangier, Morocco, earns one the right to say he's been to the same continent that has born the likes of Idi Amin, Nelson Mandela, and Tarzan.

First-time travelers would be wise to get their feet wet in Cape Town, South Africa, the wealthiest nation on the continent. The modern, charming port city would not send tourists into shock after the long 17-hour flight from America. (Who, disorientated by jet lag, would want to immediately visit a Zulu village, or be thrust into an open-air safari vehicle?). Cape Town harbor, near the meeting point of the Atlantic and Indian Oceans, is breathtakingly beautiful and ranks with Rio de Janeiro's harbor as one of the Seven Natural Wonders of the World. Spending three or four days at a hotel near the city's vibrant Waterfront district is the perfect way to get one's bearings.

WHERE THE ATLANTIC MEETS THE INDIAN OCEAN. SOUTH AFRICA

Years ago, within an hour of checking into our hotel on my first visit to Cape Town, I stuck my head out the room's window to admire Table Mountain and breathe in the ocean air. Funny, I thought looking at the modern buildings around me, Africa hardly *appears* exotic. Then a bird with purple plume and golden eyes flew by and landed on an eave. It cocked its head and gave me the once over, and with a shimmy and an "eeaghh!" took to the air, making me wonder how such a creature could survive in this cosmopolitan city. The answer, of course, is because we are talking about *Africa,* where, one learns quickly, nature's beauty trumps modern marvels, and indigenous creatures coexist with man, albeit tenuously. South Africa offers something for everybody, which can't be said about many other African nations.

Shopping, dining, and hotel accommodations are superb. Along with Kruger National Park, the largest game reserve in the world (about the size of Vermont), the country boasts some of the best private safari lodges. The beauty of the coast is beyond words, with its own marine "big game," including migrating blue whales, great white sharks, barking seals, and even braying Cape penguins. On the Atlantic Ocean side of the country (in the Western Transvaal), South Africa's coastal region is filled with sweeping sand dunes, stretching into Namibia. East of the Cape of Good Hope, the region boasts dreamy beach towns like Wilderness, a favorite honeymoon spot whose spectacular coastline director David Lean captured in his film, *Ryan's Daughter.* Port Elizabeth, Durban—these ports are the jewels of South Africa's Indian Ocean and subtropical Eastern Transvaal region.

Getting to Port Elizabeth from Cape Town is half the fun, as one crosses the Garden Route, so named for the scenic drive past Mossel Bay, Knysna, George, and other settlements founded by the Dutch. South Africa today is like the United States was in the mid-twentieth century—a kinder, gentler nation, to borrow the words of George H. Bush. While tourists must watch for pickpockets and be on guard at all times (who is not aware of the high rate of crime in South Africa?), the relative lack of traffic there, the homey mom-and-pop stores, and the politeness of the people remind many senior Americans of the Eisenhower years. Visit South Africa, and you would swear it is 1959.

As jaded as we are with new technology, we react like kids when, outside Cape Town, we come across street signs that read, "Baboons Crossing," or when we ride ostriches in Oudtshoorn. Typically, a tour of the country features a visit to a Zulu village, or *kraal*. Zulus were the country's mighty black warriors, and they make up the majority of the population. Some Americans—mostly male—are startled to find female Zulus topless in their native kraals, attired only in wrap-around skirts. It is amusing to hear the tourist husband order his wife to quickly snap a photo of him standing next to these women, as if there was a chance in hell the image would later adorn the family Christmas card. To these men, visiting a Zulu *kraal* is often the highlight of their entire African trip.

TRYING TO FIGURE OUT WHERE I SHOULD LOOK.
ZULU VILLIAGE, SOUTH AFRICA

For whatever reason, game drives in South Africa are conducted in open-air vehicles, while in Kenya and Tanzania they are done in vans with pop-up roofs. Both modes of transportation work, as each allows shutterbugs to get very close to animals. None of the coveted Big Five—rhino, elephant, lion, leopard, or Cape buffalo—are "spooked" by motor vehicles. Guides will tell you this is because the game has learned that safari wagons pose no threat to them. Interestingly enough, so many generations of animals have been exposed to these vehicles, newborns instinctively know they are not in harm's way when one crammed with camouflage-clad tourists rumbles up to them.

In open-air vehicles, some of which can accommodate up to a dozen people, a rifle-toting game spotter sits in the front of the car in case a lion decides to make a meal of Grandpa and Nana Jones, who sometimes shout and frenetically search through their backpacks for misplaced film. Spotters know that animals regard motorized vans and wagons as one entity; if the beasts discern, when there is commotion inside, that the vehicles are transporting human bonbons, there is a chance they could narrow their eyes, lick their chops and pounce. (While on safari, we once encountered a lion feeding on a fallen springbok. "How fast could he jump into our car?" I whispered to the guide. "About three seconds," was the answer). Under the circumstances, Africa is a destination that when clients ask if there is a lot of walking involved, I can truthfully answer, "Not much."

Incidentally, animal experts will tell you not to wear brightly colored clothes on safaris, especially red. Look at the affect that color has on bulls. And—please—Chanel Number Five has *no* place on a game drive. Leave your fragrances at home, ladies. Far from attracting beasts (other than perhaps the Zulu chief), scented perfume *repels* animals.

Some people believe that to truly experience Africa, one must stay in tents. This would scare the hell out of me, not so much out of fear of tiptoeing out of my tent in the middle of the night to use the porta-potty, but of being bit by mosquitoes. Mosquitoes in Africa transmit malaria and yellow fever, and even if one is immunized before a trip, it is disconcerting to hear their high-pitched whine once the Coleman lantern is out. Mosquitoes don't like cold temperatures, and because hotels and lodges are air conditioned, the threat of being bitten indoors is lessened. Tents are for kids, yet some of the most expensive adult safaris feature canvas accommodations and dig-your-own toilets. Go figure.

WHEN THE MASAI TRIBE STANDS, LALO SQUATS;
AND WHEN LALO SQUATS...KENYA

Typically, vacations to Africa are expensive, which is ironic because traveling to Black African countries—Kenya, Zimbabwe, Zambia, Botswana, Tanzania, Namibia, and others—offers something money can't buy: poverty. A selection of first class and deluxe hotels and lodges *does* exist, but life outside the guarded gates of these places is poor. This is not to say Americans will experience the terrible sights depicted on TV (flies covering faces, malnourished pot-bellied babies), because tourist roads do not lead to those sad places; but the infrastructure (unpaved roads, basic services) and housing, including shanty towns and *rondavals* (round structures with straw-thatched roofs), are testaments to poverty. Still, surprisingly, the locals smile and wave as you pass by. People may not have many material possessions in Black Africa, but they appear happy.

None of which means anything to many Americans, who sometimes grouse about delayed flights, lines at the borders, substandard buses, and lodges without satellite TV. Tourists afflicted with globetrots whine about everything from the hard seats on Kenya safari wagons to the quality of local vintages in South Africa's Winelands, and from the punctuality of transfers in Zimbabwe to the accents of Botswana guides. I've had people gripe about not seeing rhinos in the Masai Mara, and others complain about slot machines being tight in Swaziland casinos. One traveler even thought he'd be humorous, ordering turkey for dinner in Kenya and telling his waiter, "I want my meat dark, like you."

In third world countries--and name one in Africa that isn't--this is my advice (other than "roll with it" when things don't operate as you would have hoped): play like there's no tomorrow and don't be afraid to mingle with the locals or get dirty. Eat native foods, soak in the environment and in doing so, appreciate how lucky you are to live where you do. At the end of the day, after being exposed to sometimes less than sanitary conditions and exotic animals and dusty safari wagons, retire to the safety and comfort of a nice *hotel*. I don't necessarily mean the Peninsula or Ritz Hotel, which you won't find in Africa in any case; but to at least a good four-star property with hot water, fresh food (served usually outdoors "boma" style), and—most importantly—a lounge where, over a drink, you and friends can gather and talk about all you have experienced. When the trip ends, you will say to yourself, *That* was truly a great vacation.

TRYING TO BLEND IN WITH THE NATIVES
AT BOMA CEREMONY IN ZIMBABWE

Dining al fresco in Africa is enjoyable in the central and southern nations (I'd stick to eating indoors in northern Muslim countries, preferably at a reputable hotel). Sitting outdoors around a campfire and sampling pots of native vegetables and traditional fare, along with grilled crocodile, warthog, or buffalo, makes for quite a memorable "boma" evening. The *best* attractions in Africa, in fact, are outdoors. Thundering Victoria Falls stretching from Zimbabwe to Zambia, all those game drives, wandering Masai tribesmen wrapped in red cloth, Table Mountain, the monuments of Egypt, and the exotic bazaars and souks--these are all outdoors. Even in Madagascar, the oldest island in the world off Mozambique, the star of the country is the lemur, a monkey-like creature only accessible through nature walks.

At Zanzibar in Tanzania, the open-air spice market is where the action is, and the ruins of the slave trade are also located outdoors. Ditto with that country's Ngorongoro Crater, whose water basin attracts big game

YOU CAN'T SAY WE DIDN'T WARN YOU

The best hotels and lodges in Africa boast outdoor watering holes for animals, where, while one sips a drink from the bar at sunset, he can gaze at rhino, giraffe, elephants, and other game doing likewise. Places like famous Treetops Lodge in Kenya, where Elizabeth II allegedly went up a princess during her honeymoon and came down a queen after learning her father had died, are built directly over watering holes.

Guests spend most of the night outside, glued to viewing platforms where they watch all the action below. Even when they finally retire to their rooms, they have the option of being awakened with the sound of a buzzer when any of the Big Five appear to quench their thirst—or sate their appetite.

Don't travel to Africa for its great museums and do not expect to find tons of shopping malls except in South Africa and architectural wonders (the Pyramids notwithstanding). The beauty of the continent is found outdoors, in nature. Africa is a *living* museum.

Northern Muslim countries in Africa and the Middle East—Morocco, Egypt, Jordan, Tunisia, Oman, the United Arab Emirates, and other nations stretching to Turkey (which is not even on the African continent) offer similar fare: unadorned mosques, calls (wailings) to prayer blared over speakers from towering minarets; segregation of sexes; men attired in stained caftans bullshitting with each other while sucking on tangled water pipes, barking carpet salesmen, gold souks, and animated haggling at open air markets. Men are ubiquitous while women, poor things, are scarcely to be seen. Heavy, noisy traffic (impatient Muslims love to lean on their horns) await tourists in Cairo and in other big cities. Note the lack of flowerboxes and public parks, and good luck finding a lawn in any Islamic nation. Dust covers *everything*, including people: hygiene in the Arab world leaves a lot to be desired, as anyone can observe from inside his touring bus.

Thinking, along with morality and values—is (let us be polite) "different" than in the western world. Tribalism is one reason, religion is of course a second, and tradition is still another. A trip to a Muslim country for many westerners can be scary.

So, what attracts Americans to these lands? For some, the answer is to see the historical sites, although many of them are disappointing.

The scattered remains of Carthage, for example, in Tunisia hardly constitute a "must see" journey. Ditto with what is left of ancient Alexandria, Egypt. A day trip to the famous Kasbah in Tangier, Morocco, is sufficient for most Americans to get a taste of Muslim life. (Why on earth Malcolm Forbes bought a house in filthy Tangier is a mystery—rumor has it, young men were readily available).

Some archaeological sites are indeed awe-inspiring—Petra, for example, in Jordan, and the Pyramids and Sphinx at Giza** as well as Egypt's Nile temples.

*Combining a tour of Israel with any of its neighboring countries is truly an eye-opening experience, because the Holy Land is verdant, clean, and—not being Muslim--more western. Drivers in Israel don't toss garbage out their car windows; horns are at a minimum; men wear Levis, not caftans, and stroll with smartly dressed women. Remarkably, before 1947, Israel—then known as the territory of Palestine—was as arid as Egypt, Jordan, and Syria are even today. What immigrants to Israel have accomplished is wondrous: through sheer hard work, much of it done by hand, the former desert wasteland is now a fertile garden.

**My own best memory of Egypt? On a visit to the country decades ago, aboard a Princess cruise, two days were spent in the Land of Pharaohs. Instead of taking shore excursions, Lalo and i hopped a taxi in the port of Alexandria and told the friendly English-speaking driver to "show me Egypt." After visiting the sites of his city, including where the Lighthouse once stood (an Ancient Wonder of the World), the driver revved up his car, slipped into his stereo a cassette of Slim Whitman's Greatest Hits, and like a camel in heat we raced toward Cairo. You haven't lived until you approach the Great Pyramids of Giza in a cloud of dust with "I Remember You" wailing from your cab.

But why all the fuss about Dubai? Reams of publicity have been written and broadcast about the architectural marvels of the overrated Arab emirate, but in comparison to the fantastic hotels and glitz on the Strip in Las Vegas, Dubai is half baked without the casinos. Few "wonders" in Dubai are accessible to the general public, whether it is purportedly the world's tallest hotel (Burj Al Arab), where one must have a restaurant reservation to even get into the lobby (a lunch buffet will set one back about $200), or the highest office building in the world, the Burj Dubai. Forget about driving onto the famous islands shaped like palm trees or the world—they are either heavily guarded or not yet finished. The city's gigantic theme parks have yet to be built. That leaves Ski Dubai, the indoor ski complex—complete with snow--inside the Mall of the Emirates. Yeah, that's interesting—for about ten minutes.

Dubai's gold souk is nothing compared to the Grand Bazaar in Istanbul. Turkey, out of all the Muslim nations, offers Westerners a number of interesting sites. The country's ancient remains of Ephesus, a favorite cruise port stop, are enjoyed more than all the sites in Egypt by A.C.T. travelers. Ephesus at one time rivaled Rome as a commercial port, and the remains of the Temple of Artemis, one of the original Seven Wonders of the World is nearby. Anthony and Cleopatra honeymooned here, and when the apostle John invited Mary, mother of Jesus, to talk about her son at the still intact amphitheater—which held up to 25,000 people--so many Ephesians showed up that the local merchants rioted. Mary literally fled to the hills and presumably died there. Her recently discovered mountain home has been visited by a series of Popes and is today a holy pilgrimage site. (St. John, sans Mary, escaped to the Greek island of Patmos, where he wrote *Revelation*).

Cappadocia and the natural mineral baths at Pamukkale in Turkey fascinate tourists, but its famous mosques—Hagia Sofia and the Blue Mosque—disappoint, because unlike the treasury of art found inside great Christian churches, depictions of humans and animals are not allowed in the Muslim religion; therefore, the places are fairly bare. There are no pulpits, pews, or stained rose windows in mosques—just lots of geometric designs, often on tile, and plenty of floor space to accommodate prayer rugs. Mosques are self-same; whether it is the Great Mosque in Cairo or modern ones built in the Emirates, everything under the plain round domes is fairly austere. See one mosque, and you've seen them all.

Africa, then, like the other six continents, offers a mixed bag of tricks and treats. From its minority white-skinned citizens of the southern regions to its black majority in the central countries and the brown-skinned northern Muslim nations, Africa is a lopsided United States in terms of ethnicity. For American tourists, the differences are immense, not only in terms of culture and religion, but also because of those exotic animals and values system. In some countries, cattle and goats are more important to an Afrikaner than local currency—or even human beings (wives are often bought with cows). In others, notably Sudan and Mauritania, Arab Muslims still enslave people.

One of the most revealing conversations I ever had was on a plane in Kenya, with the manager of a leading African tour company. The man was Caucasian and was a native of Nairobi. He feared that because of the encroaching human population, elephants would be wiped out on the continent within 50 years. He explained that one could not simply relocate an elephant from the Serengeti to, say, Kruger Park in South Africa, where it would be protected, because the elephant would die of loneliness. Elephants are family-oriented and could not survive being separated from their clan. The entire herd of elephants would have to be moved, which would be cost prohibitive because transporting even one by air would cost about $50,000.

All of this made me wonder.

"There are starving people in Africa," I said, using the old cliché. "Instead of spending that money to move an elephant, wouldn't you rather see it go to feed *them*?"

"No," he answered without hesitation. "The $50,000 is better spent on saving the elephant. Life in Africa is hard and always has been. Human misery and death will continue long after the elephants are extinct." I suppose one would have to live there for a while to comprehend his sentiments.

A.C.T. BALLOON RIDE OVER THE GREAT MIGRATION. KENYA

THE GREAT PYRAMID OF GIZA AND SPHINX (CAIRO'S MUST-SEE SITES)

AUSTRALIA

NEW ZEALAND

&

OCEANIA

AUSTRALIA, NEW ZEALAND, AND OCEANIA

"Visiting the Lands Down Under."

"Americans top the list of worst-behaved travelers in a LivingSocial survey of 5,600 respondents, 4,000 of whom were Americans. Other respondents were in Australia, Canada, Ireland, and the U.K. But even U.S. respondents named their compatriots as the worst travelers from a list of 16 nationalities. (Canadians and Australians also put Yanks in the No. 1 spot)." --**Jayne Clark, *USA Today*, March 2, 2012**

The worst thing about Australia is the long flight it takes to get there, something like 16 hours from Los Angeles. Most people know that flights to Asia and Australia departing from the West Coast are shorter than flights from the East, and conversely, flying from JFK to Europe and Africa is quicker than flying from LAX. Miami wins the derby when it comes to shortest flights to Central and South America. Anyway, traveling from California to Australia seems never-ending, but the journey back is about three hours less, thanks to favorable winds. We suggest packing a copy of *War and Peace* in your carry-on.

The best thing about Australia, an island continent as big as the United States, is its beach communities, although the old *Pan*

American Airlines World Guide implores visitors "to visit at least part of the interior and not cling to the coastal cities." Okay, but jumping a plane to experience Ayers Rock in the Northern Territory, situated 275 miles southwest of Alice Springs in the center of the country, will set you back about $1,500 when all the residual charges are tallied. I have yet to hear anyone rave about visiting Ayers Rock, a whale-shaped stone mountain rising from the desert that only occasionally glows red at sunrise and sunset. For less money, one might prefer to head to Utah and spend a week on a houseboat in Lake Powell, which is surrounded by red sandstone boulders and gigantic edifices.

Sydney, the oldest colony (1788) in Australia and capital of New South Wales, could very well be the loveliest city in the world. The nightlife and restaurants, shopping, theater, and music scenes are tops. There is an energy in Sydney that Australia's other cities lack: nearby Canberra, the country's capital, and seat of the federal government, is as dull as Brazil's legislative capital, Brasilia, a similarly planned community. Perth, in sparsely populated Western Australia, the largest state, is the size of San Francisco but is without the—what? — *joi de vivre* and cable cars climbing halfway to the stars. Being on the Indian Ocean, Perth is stifling during the summer months. Adelaide (South Australia), Brisbane (Queensland), Darwin, Tasmania (!)— these places don't measure up to vibrant Sydney, whose attractions make the long flight from the States worthwhile, starting with its famous Opera House.

SYDNEY, AUSTRALIA (ALWAYS A POPULAR DESTINATION)

We will NOT list all the things to do in Sydney, other than encourage newcomers to experience the metropolis by land *and* sea. To truly appreciate the beauty of the city, hop onto a boat and cruise the magnificent harbor—either on a so-called "coffee cruise" or cocktail or dinner jaunt. After sailing under the famous Harbor Bridge and passing the Opera House, your ship will cruise past spectacular waterfront homes. All the other excursions combined—to Bondi Beach and the historic Rocks district, to the outlying Australian Koala Park and Blue Mountains and Paddy's Market—cannot compare to seeing Sydney by boat.

Melbourne, capital of Victoria and second largest city in Australia, is often included in package tours of the continent, but I am not sure why. The gaiety of Sydney is not there, and Melbourne lacks the history, variety of shops, scenic harbor, and great cultural venues of her big sister. Temperatures are chillier than in Sydney, and this is a college town with lots of ivy-covered red brick buildings and eateries, including an interesting streetcar restaurant. But other than that, the main attraction is a colony of Fairy Penguins outside of town, on Phillip Island, two hours away by bus. Because the birds don't emerge from the Bass Strait on the Southern Ocean until dusk, many jet-lagged tourists instantly collapse from exhaustion after battling the hordes of tourists there.

Laid back Cairns (pronounced "Cans") in North Queensland is dubbed "Gateway to the Great Barrier Reef," or what's left of it after all the recent cyclones and debilitating effects of global warming. Subtropical in climate, Cairns has something for everybody (a cliché travel promoters relish): snorkel and dive expeditions, casinos, Aborigines, a fun train (Kuranda Railway), aerial tram rides, and—for senior citizens—Green Island, an easily accessible archipelago off the coast which offers visitors glass bottom boat cruises over the Reef, as well as beachcombing opportunities.

Tourists in Sydney can cuddle koala bears (there *must* be another verb out there) and tour the famous sail-shaped Opera House and take a day tour to the Blue Mountains. In Cairns they can experience the Great Barrier Reef and throw boomerangs with Aborigines. Together, these two cities provide visitors with enough memories to justify the long trans-Pacific flights.

Americans usually feel at home in Australia, and the reason, not surprisingly, is the freedom-loving, easy nature of the inhabitants. Both the United States and Australia were settled by Europeans who faced unfamiliar animals and terrain when they arrived. To this day, the two nations grapple with indigenous populations and share common environmental and social concerns. Americans and Australians generally shirk the pomp and circumstance of Europe; both countries prefer informal attire and lifestyles. At casinos in Sydney and Las Vegas, winning players cry out when they hit jackpots, whereas in Monte Carlo and in gambling halls in Moscow, there is a funereal silence when three 7's line up on slot machines.

America has funny characters, and with the late Crocodile Hunter, Dame Edna, and the Road Warrior, so does Australia. Both continents share a passion for democracy, and the unique geographical location of the U.S. and the Land Down Under has protected each country from foreign aggressors. Americans justifiably feel safe in Australia.

A bit stodgier are New Zealanders, affectionately known as Kiwis. Their aloofness is curious, in light of the exuberant athleticism found on both islands of the country. Auckland in the North is known, among other things, for its yacht races, while bungee jumping allegedly had its origins in Queenstown, on the South Island (the so-called land divers of Pentecost Island in Vanuatu might contest that). There is world class skiing in the New Zealand Alps, sheep sheering on both islands, and cowboy riding in the Canterbury Plains. Soccer and rugby are passions in the country—especially in matches against Australia--and champion rowing is king in Christchurch and Dunedin. One wonders, therefore, if the prim mores of the English have left their marks on Kiwi society, or if the cold weather (on the South Island, anyway) has muted the citizens' gaiety, as it has on Scandinavians. At least New Zealand's Maori people, adorned in Polynesian tattoos, appear to take life not too seriously. These days, visitors to Rotorua on the North Island are greeted by half-naked Maoris, who delight in making outrageous faces and shaking fake spears. As tourists giggle at the antics of these brown-skinned natives, white Kiwis bridle.

STEVE AND THE NATIVES IN VANUATU

LALO WITH MAORI WOMEN, NEW ZEALAND

As is the case with Australia, New Zealand is a country where Americans travel without many being stricken by globetrots. English is the official language, prices are similar to those in the U.S., and safety is seldom an issue. Some places, like lovely Christchurch, with its Avon River, refuse to shed its 1960's aura; other cities, like Auckland, are reminiscent of Boston or San Francisco. One could argue that the many natural sites of New Zealand, from the glow worm caves and geothermal geysers of the North Island to famous Milford Sound, that pristine fjord of the South, as well as the country's many lakes and rivers, are more spectacular than anything a person will experience in Australia. I've heard many Americans say they'd like to retire in New Zealand. Little wonder that the enchanted country has some of the strictest immigration laws in the world.

Both Australia and New Zealand comprise a geographical area dubbed "Oceania," commonly called the South Pacific. Here one will also find the Society Islands—Tahiti, Moorea, Bora Bora, and others comprising French Polynesia. In addition, there are Fiji, Tonga, the Cook Islands, and scores of other countries whose tourist boards try to lure travelers with idealized posters of turquoise waters, swaying palm trees, and sexy natives attired in loin cloths and coconut brassieres. Romantic images of over-the-water bungalows and spectacular sunsets inspire thousands of pasty-faced American office workers to alight from their swivel chairs and catch the first flight to Bali Hai, despite its fictitious name (in reality, that island in the musical *South Pacific* is Bora Bora, immortalized in James Michener's "Tales of the South Pacific." A popular bar named Bloody Mary's pays tribute to him there).

GOING COCONUTS IN MOOREA, FRENCH POLYNESIA

The first thing Americans utter when their plane lands in Papeete, Tahiti is, "This ain't no Honolulu," which is an understatement. The capital of Tahiti is fairly unattractive with few interesting retail stores or restaurants. Only a non-descript open-air market in Papeete is active in the mornings. Even the island's Paul Gaugin Museum lacks original paintings by the French master. We should have known something was amiss when mutinous Fletcher Christian, before setting sail to a different island, dumped overboard Tahiti's only claim to fame, breadfruit, along with Captain Bligh. Outside of a handful of black-sand beach resorts, Papeete rewards visitors with nothing but a pretty view of Moorea, an island which rivals Bora Bora as being perhaps the most beautiful in the world.

But other than snorkeling or diving, there is nothing to do in Moorea, or Bora Bora for that matter, or Raiatea or in any of the other Society Islands! The great shopping and dining opportunities offered in Hawaii do not exist on these islands, and meals are almost unaffordable (a cheeseburger with fries will set you back twenty bucks). Some of the islands are built on sharp coral reefs, which makes wading into the waters dangerous and painful; and unlike the islands in our 50th state, which have consistently pleasant weather, there is a horrific, humid wet season in Polynesia that leaves tourists sopping. It has been my observation that most seniors (especially women) do not like to get wet, which leaves out water sports and anything to do with strapping on goggles and face masks. Because there is nothing else to do but swim in Tahiti, Moorea, etc., many Americans over the age of 70 return disappointed. (Snorkelers and scuba divers, however, are enraptured with the Society Islands and consider the destination Nirvana).

Probably the best way to sample French Polynesia is by cruise ship, as meals are included, and the expense of inter-island flights are eliminated. In addition, the activities on board (gambling, concerts, and show venues) make up for the lack of things to do on land. Tranquility, of course, is exactly what *some* people seek on a vacation, but the majority of tourists "want it all," and the Society Islands (commonly referred to as Tahitian Islands) fail to provide that.

A.C.T. GROUP ARRIVES IN FIJI!

Fiji is a Melanesian group of 300 islands (also known as the Cannibal Islands) east of Polynesia. Late night entertainment there consists of watching dark natives walk over hot coals. Perhaps in recoil, the late actor Raymond Burr built a house in Viti Levu, the main island of the archipelago, and grew orchids when he retired, a far more civil pastime. His estate is open for touring, and that is good because I can't think of too much else to do in Fiji, other than

engage in underwater exploring opportunities, which the Submarine Voyage at Disneyland includes in its entrance price and is far cheaper.

I can't recommend going to the Cook Islands, either. In comparison to Rarotonga, its muddy capital, Papeete is alive and vibrant. Once again, there is little to do on the Cook Islands, other than take circle tours in discarded school buses from Biloxi. If alive, Captain James Cook, the namesake discoverer, would sue for defamation.

*A wise man once asked, "Is Hell *not* getting what you want, or is it getting what you want?" Detached hotel rooms dotting moonlit, tropical beaches of Polynesia naturally spark romantic inclinations, especially when people first arrive from the States. Paradise found; they think! On a first night in Moorea, I recall bidding good night to members of our group, watching them retire hand-in-hand to their palm-thatched quarters on the beach. The next morning, women appeared post-coital. With only radios in their rooms, however, many soon became bored. The hotel's activities consisted of crab races and burying a slaughtered pig in hot sand for a Tahitian feast that, alas, few people, after witnessing the ritual, cared to engage in. Romance apparently was all but gone a week later when, strolling past one of the rooms, I heard a wife screaming at her husband, "I don't care where you go—take up clam digging—*just find something to do and leave me alone!*" Paradise lost.

On that particular vacation in Moorea, an island excursion to Tahiti was included on the last day, departing the hotel lobby at 9 a.m. On the way to breakfast at 7:30, I was surprised to find every member of the group waiting anxiously in the lobby, afraid of missing the ferry. It reminded me that Henry Thoreau died in London, not at Walden Pond.

In 2014 Lalo and I escorted a group of 29 adventurous souls on a voyage aboard the intimate *Paul Gauguin* cruise ship to Papua New

Guinea, Vanuatu, and the Solomon Islands (also part of Oceania). The cruise ended in Fiji.

Port Moresby, capital of Papua New Guinea, was the first stop after we sailed from Cairns. "The country (PNG)," I wrote in our first newsletter to participants, "lies entirely within the tropics just south of the Equator and 100 miles north of Australia and encompasses the eastern part of New Guinea island--the second largest island in the world. With a population of over seven million, there are more than 800 distinct languages, corresponding to as many tribes." I don't mean to sound callous, but with that many tribes, when you see one native in straw garb you've seen them all. And that is what happened when we dropped anchor in Samarai Island and on Bougainville Island, where natives warmly greeted us on the pier "in the traditional Melanesian way--with singing and dancing." Ditto at Port Vila on the Isle of Efate, Vanuatu's most populous island—black natives dancing with spears and wearing what looked like hay. I wonder if we Americans all look alike in their eyes.

Travel affects people in a variety of ways, of course, and visiting sites where American soldiers have sacrificed their lives often moves me to tears. Such was the case when we visited the memorial at Guadalcanal in the Solomon Islands. During World War II more than 1,600 Americans died at Guadalcanal and 4,000 were wounded; the Japanese lost 24,000 men, many from starvation.

Islands in paradise? Yes, travel posters promoting fun under the sun in Polynesia, Melanesia, and Oceania do attract tourists. But while on vacation, stumbling across remnants of the bloody past are poignant reminders of the real world we live in.

CENTRAL AND SOUTH AMERICA

"Everything south of San Diego is Mexico."

- Anonymous, overheard at a party in Los Angeles

That cynical comment, in a figurative sense, would make a great debate resolution. The defense team would have fun pointing out the many similarities between Mexico and Central and South American countries:

1) Spanish influence. From churches to terra cotta roofs and Moorish tiled patios and bubbling fountains, the Iberian Peninsula has left a strong mark on every aspect of architecture in nations below the U.S.

2) Beaches and mountains. No other country can *quite* match Mexico's diverse terrain, but Central America straddles the same bodies of water--the Pacific Ocean and Caribbean Sea--and the Sierra Madre range, which forms a spine down Mexico, attracting tourists to its colonial cities and to the Copper Canyon, can be compared to South America's spectacular Andes mountains, with historical cities like Cuzco, Quito, and Santiago.

3) Lack of a substantial Middle Class. Most Mexicans and people south of that country are either rich or sub-middle class, which in the United States would pass as poor.

4) **Lifestyle.** Though money is, of course, vital, it seemingly is *not* the key to happiness for Mexicans, Central Americans, and South Americans. Family life and "smelling life's roses" are more important, as evidenced in cultural traditions like siestas and family functions. There is a Spanish expression, "*Manana* is the busiest day of the week," suggesting there is no rush to get things done in Latin countries (and as I described in the Europe chapter about my frustrating experience on the French Riviera, the maxim is not just restricted to Latin American countries).

TULUM, MEXICO

While no sensible person will contend that Mexico and, say, Argentina is indistinguishable, there ARE cultural, historical, and social similarities shared by them and, in fact, all nations within the Asian, Latin, Slavic, African, and Germanic classifications of people. Cuisine, for example, is almost identical in all of Hispania: beans (refried in Mexico, black everywhere else), rice, grilled meats, seafood, and simple breads or tortillas. These foods are not common in German-speaking or Slavic countries, where potatoes, cabbage, heavy soups, sausage, and roast meats rule.

Boardwalks, or *malecons,* are beloved in Latin America and are crowded with families, who often stroll on them past the midnight hour. Try finding *malecons* in Moscow or Frankfurt. Hispanics enjoy being outdoors, a passion not particularly shared by gringos. When was the last time you spotted a family other than Latinos having a picnic in a public park? Obesity in America has become chronic in part because we prefer to stay indoors, close to our computers and Nintendo games.

Travelers from the States who venture "south of San Diego" usually do so with trepidation. Stories of crime, revolutions, and Third World conditions scare seniors. The phrase, "Don't drink the water" had its origins in Mexico, after all; and what, globetrotters sarcastically ask, is there to see in Central American banana republics other than bananas?

Plenty, as thousands of ex-patriots would answer from their beachfront homes in Costa Rica and Panama. Approaching from the sea, Panama City's skyline now resembles New York's, with high rise hotels and apartments, casinos, and classy stores. There is an energy and youthfulness in the capital of Panama that was not there when General Noriega ruled the country. His face in the newspapers has been replaced by Donald Trump and other building tycoons.

Costa Rica, a thriving democracy, has the reputation of being the "Switzerland of Central America" because of the country's high level of literacy and history of peace. There the similarity ends. Windows on homes are sealed with bars, chickens wander the highways, and the country is poor by U.S. standards. The fabled natural beauty of Costa Rica is there, but the volcanoes, lakes, and jungles of Guatemala are more impressive. Those pretty beaches in Costa Rica are often pretty humid.

I also have a hard time raving about non-descript Honduras and poverty-riddled Belize. Although I've never set foot in El Salvador, I am inclined to believe a taxi driver in Ecuador who, when asked what there is to see that country, answered "Not much." Central American jungle nations start to all look alike—or does that smack of what the party guest said about Mexico and all that is south of San Diego, California?

Guatemala, my personal favorite Central American nation, boasts ancient Mayan ruins like Tikal, as well as wonderful Indian markets. With its cobblestoned streets, Antigua, a UNESCO World Heritage colonial town outside of the capital, Guatemala City, is storybook in flavor.

In South America, I've traveled to parts of Brazil, Uruguay, Colombia, Argentina, Chile, Peru, Ecuador, and peered into Paraguay. I've stayed at an Amazon lodge and have been face-to-face with a blue-footed booby on the Galapagos Islands. In assessing these destinations, let's take 'em one by one.

Brazil has three main attractions: its beaches, the Amazon River, and Iguassu Falls. Few tourists are interested in going to its planned, boring inland capital, Brasilia. Because there is a paucity of anything cultural to experience in Sao Paulo, that sprawling metropolis is also out. If for nothing else, then, many Americans are willing to pay for a Brazilian tourist visa to simply see Rio de Janeiro and its famous sites, including Sugar Loaf Mountain, Corcovado (Christ statue), Copacabana Beach, and the girls of Ipanema. Some misguided souls go during Carnival (*Carnaval*), that boisterous celebration during Lent when pickpockets and muggers clean up for the rest of the year. If ever there was a season *not* to go to Rio, it would be at Carnaval time.

Rio de Janeiro is seductive, for sure, and samba music is just part of the allure. The designs on the mosaic *malecon* on Copacabana Beach beckon you to nearby Ipanema, and the sexiness of the Portuguese-speaking Brazilian men makes spinsters blush. We don't need to elaborate on the effect native women in "dental floss" bikinis have on male tourists (ever see the film, *Blame It on Rio*?). Going to *churriachia* restaurants to feast on barbecued meats is wonderful, and few can drink just one *mojito*, Brazil's refreshing cocktail. Forget New York City; Rio de Janeiro is the city that never sleeps, and its beautiful harbor is listed as one of the Seven Natural Wonders of the World.

Iguassu Falls borders Argentina and southern Brazil and is often compared to Victoria Falls in Zimbabwe. Made up of hundreds of cataracts, the region is good for a one or two-night stay, and in our mind the Hotel Cataratas on the Brazilian side offers the best accommodations, because it is the only hotel situated inside the actual Iguassu National Park. The trail abutting the Falls is only 100 feet from the lobby entrance.

THE CATARATAS HOTEL AT IGUASSU FALLS, BRAZIL

Iguassu is surrounded by tropical jungles and rainforest, so it is common to see parrots and macaws flying overhead as you walk the catwalks bordering the Falls. *Shotover* boats race up the Iguassu River, taking brave visitors to the base of the cascades to get soaked. The experience is wonderful and invigorating, although you wouldn't know it by the reaction of globetrotters who bitch about the lack of a banister on the steps leading to the boat, or how the drenching spray ruined their hairdos. I even have had clients refuse to leave their hotel to view the Falls, complaining of exhaustion after the four-hour flight from Rio. Others have griped about the old age of the classic and newly restored Cataratas hotel, now owned and operated by the Orient Express Company.

*Paraguay is one of those countries that is almost too dangerous to visit. It is a hotbed of terrorist groups. Currently, Bolivia also falls in that category. Honduras is once again in turmoil, and who wants to explore bankrupt, socialist Venezuela?

More than its modern capital, Montevideo, Uruguay should promote the town of Colonia, a World Heritage Site. Colonia is the oldest Spanish-founded city in that country, and its historical past is evident as you stroll its cobble-stoned streets. Communities like Colonia, Uruguay—along with Antigua in Guatemala and Trinidad in Cuba and Cuzco in Peru and even old town in touristy Puerto Vallarta, Mexico--are living museums that are endearing to visitors.

Colombia has a reputation for kidnappings and drugs, so except for the cruise port of Cartagena, the country's second largest city (only Bogota is bigger), not many Americans venture there. During the Spanish Inquisition, Cartagena was where the looted Inca gold was packed and shipped across the Atlantic. Remnants of the Spanish occupancy—a number of crumbling forts and walls—still exist, as does an interesting colonial section of town with military statues, outdoor restaurants, and an atmosphere akin to the old Jewish section of Seville, Spain. American tourists should skip overpriced shore excursions and take a cab directly to the old historic section, where they can safely wander the neighborhood, browse the shops and galleries, and enjoy a native meal in one of the restaurants or cafes.

Outside the city limits of Cartegena, one can get a sense of how local Colombians live by taking a tour of the mangrove tunnels. Mangrove trees form natural tunnels in saline water, in regions teeming with blue herons and other natural wildlife. Houses around the mangroves are dilapidated but the residents, many descendants of African slaves, appear happy in their environs.

Part of Iguassu Falls, as we mentioned, lies in Argentina, so if Argentina but not Brazil is on your itinerary, take the opportunity to witness the spectacle. The same setup as Brazil exists—catwalks and trails take you to the Falls—and a very well-situated Sheraton Hotel handles many American groups who typically spend one or two nights there before continuing to Buenos Aires, the capital.

The capital of Argentina is indeed cosmopolitan (the adjective every tour catalogue uses to describe the city), and it is true that Buenos Aires possesses a European flair manifested in its architecture, wide avenues, and pedestrian shopping streets. I never tire of playing tourist in Buenos Aires, going to tango shows and gaucho ranches to see the cowboys perform. It is one of the few cities in the world where I urge people to visit a cemetery, famous Recoleta, where Juan and Eva Peron are buried, along with other notable families. Some of the ornate and spacious tombs and crypts there can pass for small houses.

Besides the expected succulent steaks and grilled poultry, Argentina, because of generations of immigrants from Italy, offers visitors excellent Italian cuisine. For me, however, Argentine *beets* are the finest in the world! It sounds crazy, but the texture and sweetness of beets in the nation famous for grilled meats and vintage wine is unbeatable (forgive the pun).

From the austere beauty of Patagonia to the south and the fertile winelands at the foot of the Andes in the north, Argentina stretches some 3,000 miles. Once again, many Americans have been fairly spoiled in their own country with wine tastings and mountain and lake spectacles, so I advise spending about five days in the capital (while there, take that day trip to Colonia, Uruguay) and also flying to Iguassu Falls. Then go somewhere else. Anywhere, that is, except Chile.

Santiago, Chile is a dull capital that offers nothing but examples of the first balconies every constructed on the continent, introduced by the Spanish. If you've been to Alaska or Norway, the Chilean fjords are passé, and if you have visited Napa Valley or other wineries around the world, Maipo Valley is a disappointment. Wines in Chile are superior to any other country in South America, however, and are affordable. And the most delicious sea bass in the world can be ordered at the restaurants lining Valparaiso harbor.

Easter Island, the most isolated island in the world (they say), also belongs to Chile and would appeal to anyone interested in discovering its enormous stone *moai* statues, those three and four-story carved faces dotting the island. Thousands of archaeological sites can be explored on Easter Island, a.k.a. Rapa Nui; but don't look for discotheques and Rodeo Drive. After visiting Santiago for two days, go for the tranquility, lack of tourists, and friendly Polynesian people. The mystical island is hauntingly beautiful.

LALO SALUTING STATELY MOAI STATUES ON EASTER ISLAND

SNORKELING AT ROATAN ISLAND, HONDURAS

It seems like everyone who has heard of Machu Picchu wants to travel to Peru and visit the alleged "lost city" of the Incas. Seniors worry about the altitude, though, because at 7,000 feet, trudging over the tiered levels would, in their minds, take the wind out of a mule. Little do they realize that from the train station below the site, buses transport visitors right to the entrance gates of Machu Picchu. From there, an easy walk of about 100 feet along a straight path delivers them to the center of the complex with 360-degree postcard vistas. In actuality, visiting this most famous Inca site is a piece of cake.

Cuzco is another story. Many people have never heard of the original capital of Peru, but at 12,400 feet high in the Andes, Cuzco is one place that literally takes your breath away. Natives drink tea made from coca leaves (the same stuff cocaine comes from) just to calm the stomach, which commonly is made queasy by lack of sufficient oxygen. Even the very fit Spanish conquistador Francisco Pizarro could not breathe in Cuzco, so he razed the capital and established a new one in Lima, at sea level.

Little remains of Cuzco except enormous foundation stones and walls of precision-cut boulder that fit as tight as those three-ton blocks that make up the Pyramids of Giza. Boulders, coca tea, and rainbow flags*--that's what comes to mind when I think of Cuzco.

Globetrotters complain that there's nothing worth doing in Lima except resting up before the flight to Cuzco, but I disagree. The Gold Museum is one of the finest museums of its kind in the Americas, containing pre-Columbian art and many priceless gold artifacts that were hidden from the Spanish looters. Just setting foot inside the museum is a dazzling experience—I could spend a day there, playing Midas.

From Lima, one might consider taking a luxury Cruz del Sur bus to Nazca, to fly over the mysterious Nazca Lines. No one has a definitive answer as to how the 300 or so enormous rock outlines of animals and designs—discernable only from above--were created. If that does not interest you, fly to Iquitos on the Amazon River and spend three days at an Amazon lodge.

*A rainbow flag proudly waves on every street corner in Cuzco, and it's not because the former Incan capital is the sister city of gay-friendly San Francisco (it's not) or West Hollywood. The rainbow is merely the official symbol of Cuzco.

Earlier we pointed out that the Amazon River was one of the reasons people travel to Brazil. Manaus, in that country, is usually the starting place of an Amazon cruise. The world's largest river, however, actually starts in Peru, from melted snow waters of the Andes. The best places to stay on the river have no electricity, like the Sinchicuy Amazon Lodge a couple hours downstream from the port city of Iquitos. Bright lights and the noise of televisions, electric blenders, and air conditioners repel native wildlife; therefore, if you want to genuinely experience the Amazon River and its natural environs skip the comfortable eco-resorts and cruise boats and stay two or three nights at a lodge. Your naturalist guide will take you fishing for piranhas, searching for pink dolphins, and canoeing through waters with six-feet lily pads. You will visit Amazon tribes on the banks of the river, where you can hold anaconda snakes, sloths, monkeys, and other animals indigenous to the area, and take nature walks through the jungle. You will discover how people survive in the Amazon rain forest and when it's all over, you will marvel at how YOU survived the experience. For two nights and three days, you may feel like you're in boot camp, but the indelible memories of the sounds of animals at night, of dining on piranha that you caught earlier, of the monkeys outside the door of your quarters, of the parrots and fluorescent Amazon butterflies will stay with you for the rest of your life.

LALO WITH AMAZON NATIVES CARRYING BLOW GUNS AND BEADS

The first animal you are likely to see on the Galapagos Islands is a dairy cow. Planes full of excited tourists land every two hours on a deserted U.S. landing strip on Baltra Island, a tiny chunk of floating desert in the Galapagos archipelago chain situated 600 miles off the coast of Ecuador. From there, they take a bus to a nearby ferry and, after piling their luggage onto the boat's roof, make a quick crossing to Santa Cruz Island, the only one in the Galapagos that boasts seven climate zones. Within 20 minutes, tourists go from cacti to banana trees. Ten minutes further up the road, they wish they had brought their sweaters, the temperature has dropped so dramatically. All the while, they are giddy with excitement—Where are those exotic animals, like giant turtles? Was that a Darwin Finch that flew in front of us? *I think I just spotted an iguana!*

In fact, it was probably a hog. The highway on Santa Cruz that leads to Puerto Arroyo and Finch Bay, where most U.S. tourists board their bobbing boats, is the only paved road that fully dissects any of the islands. En route, transfer buses whiz past farms where livestock grazes in pastures. Tortoises are fiercely protected in the Galapagos (a faux pas would be asking a waiter for turtle soup), hence the wire fences alongside the roads. Most of the animals on the islands are creatures of the sea—marine iguanas, seals and sea lions, red sally-footed crabs, hammerhead sharks, sea turtles, and countless varieties of marine birds. But the enormous turtles, some of which were only recently alive when the famous evolutionist Charles Darwin observed them 160 years ago, are the biggest draw to sightseers, who can get up close to them at the Tortoise Breeding Center and the Charles Darwin Research Station on Santa Cruz Island.

IMAGINE THE TURTLE SOUP....GALAPAGOS

Americans tend to pay upwards of $8,000 to experience the Galapagos on yachts and a handful of older cruise ships for three, four, and five days, dropping anchor off islands named Floreana, Isabella, and Bartolome. They tender to shore and see with few exceptions (penguins being one) the same animals that are on Santa Cruz Island. Europeans balk at spending that much money and prefer to unpack once and nest at seaside hotels on Santa Cruz, which is in the center of the archipelago. From there, they take day excursions to the other islands at a fraction of the cost. Either way, the experience of getting up close to animals in the wild without having them flinch is a genuine thrill. Being forever protected, Galapagos creatures simply have no conception of what a predator is. Mankind could learn a lot after paying a visit to the seven Galapagos Islands, which are isolated yet linked by similar landscapes and natural life. The same can be said about the countries and peoples south of San Diego.

ANTARCTICA

"Have you got family there?"

Asked by a polite but naive teenage store clerk as she bagged my purchase of snow gloves, when I mentioned I was headed to Antarctica.

This chapter will be short, because Antarctica can be summarized by three words, each a different part of speech: **penguins, melting, and disappointing.** *Notice I did not write "frigid," as the biggest surprise was that in January, the month we boarded Orient Lines' cruise ship* Marco Polo *and sailed there from Ushuaia, Argentina, the weather was cold but not unbearable. After all, in the southern hemisphere, seasons are reversed; therefore, January was the height of summer. Note, too, that "white" was not used in my description, because contrary to what I had thought, snow covered only about half of the landscape. Lots of rocks and ground protruded from the ocean; scientists say that the way things are melting, in 50 years trees will be sprouting on the Antarctica Peninsula.*

It takes about three days to reach Antarctica by ship from the southernmost point of South America. Maybe because of the season, the waters off notorious Cape Horn were tame coming and going. By the third day, icebergs appeared outside our cabin's window, a welcome relief from the monotony of a listless and dark ocean. Almost everyone travels to Antarctica by ship, and most Americans experience just the Peninsula part of the continent (departing from

New Zealand, the continent's actual mainland is closer). On our voyage, both the Peninsula and mainland were—what? –trod upon by us cruise passengers. I cannot in truth say "explored," and therein lies the problem I have in recommending it as a "must-see" destination.

Access to Antarctica is strictly regulated by the United Nations. Our ship was only half full, not due to lack of interest, but because the amount of people allowed to traverse Antarctica was controlled and monitored; at least that is what we were told aboard the Marco Polo. Only five times during our voyage were we actually allowed to step onto shore. Once our galoshes touched land, we could do as we pleased for one hour, as long as we did not go beyond the areas roped off by the ship's crew and did not remove so much as a pebble from the ground or pet, fondle, or kick any of the penguins. And there were penguin colonies galore: Chin Strapped, Adelie, and other Gentoo varieties but no Emperor Penguins, as they are found not on the peninsula but on the mainland a thousand miles west.

At every landing, the smell of penguin guano greeted us. After climbing to the top of an icy hill and loudly saluting Antarctica with a Maria Van Trapp twirl, one member of our party skidded off the slick rocks, made slimy by penguins' droppings, and rolled down the embankment into the Weddell Sea, breaking her arm in the process. To think she survived all that and still had an appetite for lobster and Baked Alaska later that evening....

For the satisfaction of saying they've been to Antarctica, each cruise passenger typically shelled out about $5,000—the cost would be about twice that amount today--a whopping grand for each hour on shore. That's a lot of dough to play Roald Amundsen, an early explorer of the White Continent. Judging from the comments I heard aboard the Marco Polo, the whole rationale for going there was to put a final flag on their "Been There Done That" maps. Passengers, many of whom appeared to be in their 80's, quipped they had traveled everywhere else and only wanted to complete their collection of visited continents. One lady asked the ship's distinguished Antarctica expert if by fortune she might spot polar bears atop icebergs.

HAPPY CAMPERS IN ANTARCTICA

STUMBLING ACROSS WHALEBONES ON THE WHITE CONTINENT

My disappointment in Antarctica was not shared by others on the cruise. When I asked members of our group if they still would have signed up, knowing in advance that they would be spending just five hours on land after sailing for three days to get there and another three to get back, the response was unanimous: Of course! What kind of cynical question is that?! The whole experience was unforgettable! *a cruise through the inland passage of America's 49th state. You won't see any penguins, but there are at least trees as well as glaciers and bald eagles, seals, whales, and (if you're fortunate to see them) bears.*

In John LeCarre's Tinker, Tailor, Soldier, Spy, **George Smiley,** *spy extraordinaire, points out that "the more one has paid for a forgery, the more one defends it in the face of all the evidence to the contrary." I'm no psychologist, but I suspect when people sign up for an expensive holiday, they are more likely to rave about the experience afterward than those who vacation on the cheap. Rationalizing the expense, travelers to Antarctica display to their friends the red Antarctic jackets that were presented to them on the ship, as well as certificates signed by the captain proving they made the journey; and they describe how adventuresome the ordeal was with exaggerated stories of having to sit atop inflatable zodiac landing rafts in frigid waters. On our voyage, more than one senior tumbled off his raft before reaching shore, which might explain why landings are now limited to companies like Lindblad Expeditions, whose pricing includes liability coverage.*

DON'T BRING YOUR SUN LOTION

EXOTIC DESTINATIONS

EXOTIC DESTINATIONS

"Were you born in China, or have you always been Mongoloid?"

--Question posed by American tourist to our guide in Ulaanbaatar, capital of Mongolia

Soon after it was founded, Adult Customized Tours had sold London, Paris, and Rome so many times that it started offering trips to more exotic destinations, places like Antarctica, Easter Island, Myanmar, Nepal, Madagascar, Zanzibar, Fiji, the Cook Islands, Serbia, Yemen, Oman, Ecuador, Guatemala, Belize, and other non-tourist spots most people probably couldn't find on a map. Mongolia. Tibet. The tiny Baltic nations (Estonia, Latvia, Lithuania). The Canary Islands. You get the gist.

Whenever A.C.T. posted these and other exotic journeys (at least in the minds of the majority of tourists), people afflicted with globetrots inevitably reacted with hesitation before asking the usual question: "Yeah, but when are you going to Paris?" Or London. Or Rome. After a sigh and a rub of the temples, we would answer, "What month do you want to go, from which airport, and how many stars do you want to see posted next to the hotel's name?"

Trips to unusual lands, in my mind, are the most interesting, because they produce a wide range of emotions and--when the countries are *really* distant and mysterious--make one fall in love with America all over again, upon return. Just the thought of going off-the-beaten-path fills one with a sense of adventure. Travelers know in advance they will come back with great stories to share with family and friends, and that they will be perceived as real Marco Polos, rather than typical tourists with name badges strung around their necks.

MEMORIES OF EXOTICA THAT COME BACK TO US:

~ Cruising through the Suez Canal, where machine-gunners on either side--stationed 50 yards apart--guarded the vital waterway from terrorists. To those of us observing the ominous scene, the ice-carving demonstration being staged on the upper "fun deck" during the passage seemed woefully irreverent.

~ Sleeping in "gers" (a.k.a "yurts"), round tents in the Gobi Desert and in Outer Mongolia, with no private facilities and only one or two candles to lighten the way to the camp's latrines, some 50 yards away.

~ Ousting rogue monkeys from rooms at lodges in Zimbabwe and deep inside the Amazon jungle.

~ Seeing half-naked Vanuatu natives shaking their spears while dancing at their Melanesian village. Ditto Zulu women dancing topless with tribesmen wearing nothing but straw apparel at *Zulu Kral* in South Africa.

~ Watching a women's club president in one of our distinguished desert cities performing a Maria Von Trapp-like twirl on an icy slope in

Antarctica, shouting "I have arrived!" before accidentally slipping on penguin guano, falling on her ass and sliding into the icy Weddell Sea.

~ Witnessing a client lose his footing in the Zambezi River in Zambia and having to rescue him from tumbling over Victoria Falls.

~ Trying to figure out how the natives moved those heavy *moai*—the enormous Polynesian faces carved on monoliths--on Easter Island.

~ Whizzing through the Himalaya Mountains on a flight-seeing plane, getting up close to Mt. Everest.

~ Climbing to the top of Angkor Wat, Cambodia, and the Potola Palace in Tibet

~ Shaking hands of U.S. servicemen and giving thanks to them while they enjoyed R&R in the Sultanate of Oman.

~ Daring to talk politics in Tibet, Cuba, and Russia. Explaining again why we can't help someone in an oppressed land escape his country.

~ Exploring *the Hill of Crosses* in Lithuania, where over 100,000 crosses stand in defiance of former fascist regimes (Nazis, Soviets). Truly an inspirational experience!

THE INCREDIBLE HILL OF CROSSES IN LITHUANIA

"Sometimes the road less traveled is less traveled for a reason."--Jerry Seinfeld.

So, to add to some of the exotic destinations of the world: Papua New Guinea. Jordan, Morocco, and Dubai. Swaziland. The Solomon Islands. Latvia and Lithuania. India. Laos. Romania. Mauritius. Vanuatu. Easter Island. San Marino. Oxnard....You get the picture: anywhere but London, Paris, and Rome. With so many *normal* (in lack of a better word) vacation destinations out there and so few opportunities to experience them all, why would anyone want to waste the time and money visiting Serbia, Uruguay, or Laos? Having been fortunate enough to visit each of these remote places--some more exotic than others, but none a particular magnet to American tourists--perhaps I can shed light on the answer, with the help of quotations from two great writers, Kurt Vonnegut, and Albert Camus.

"Bizarre travel plans are dancing lessons from God," wrote Vonnegut, to which Camus would seem to concur when he noted that "What gives value to travel is fear." The meaning behind these pearls of wisdom can be illustrated in the following episode Lalo and I experienced in 2008, during a cruise from Rome through the Suez Canal to Dubai on the Red Sea, featuring ports of call on the Arabian Peninsula.

At the approximate time Al Qaeda moved its base from Afghanistan to Yemen, Costa Cruises* nevertheless opted to include in its Red Sea itinerary the port of Aden, the infamous Yemeni port where the *USS Cole* had been attacked in 2000, killing 17 American sailors and injuring 39 others. Lalo and I—two ignorant participants of that Costa voyage, having forgotten the *Cole* incident and being oblivious to the U.S. State Department's warning about travel to Yemen--decided to book the ship's overnight shore excursion showcasing the country's capital, a tour the cruise line sweetly named "Scenic Sana'a." We set off in a caravan of vans from Aden; only later did we learn that just two weeks prior to our ship's arrival, a similar convoy of vans carrying Belgian nuns was stopped in its track by terrorists, who promptly strafed the vehicles with machine guns. There were no survivors.

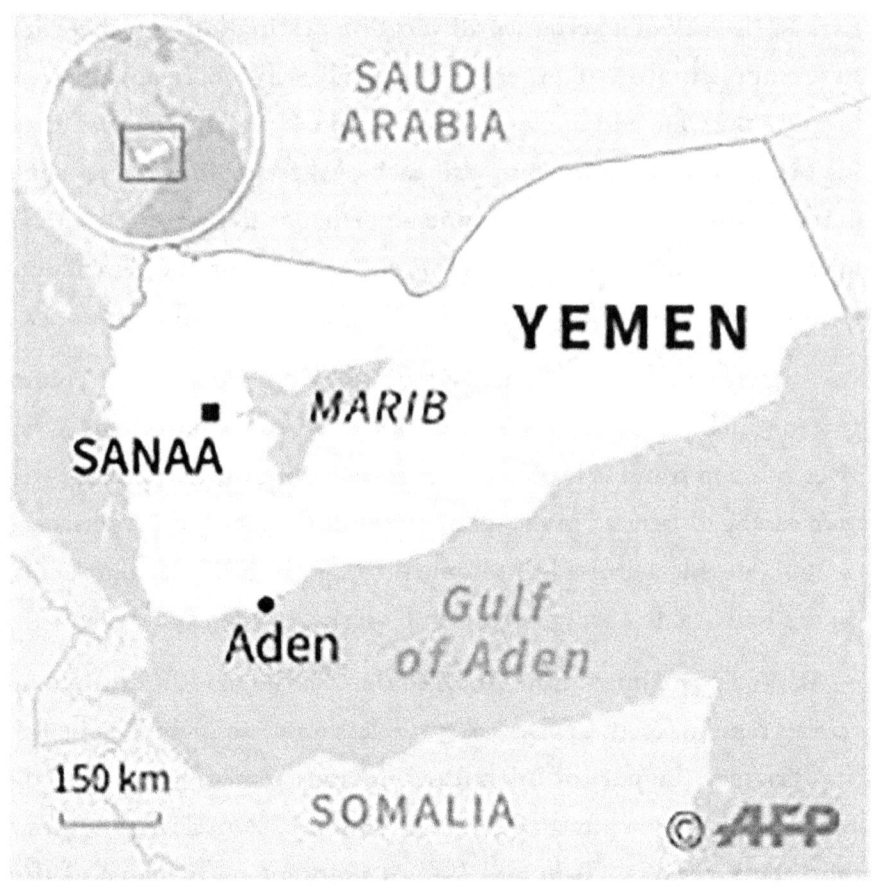

YEMEN MAP

The road trip to Sana'a followed a two-lane highway through dusty towns that highlighted the typical architecture of Yemen (brick buildings crisscrossed with white tiles). We passed lots of men garbed in dirty kaftans doing nothing but sitting and yawning, appearing stoned. And, indeed, stoned they were, as the government, we were told, condoned, and even *encouraged* the use of khat, a flowering plant that when dried and chewed, was used as a stimulant. Both khat and its cousin, marijuana, can also induce sedation, however, and by all appearances that was the affect it had on the males who gathered on street curbs and lay sprawled under trees. As our vans passed, thousands of small blue plastic bags blew to the sides of the road, testimony to how khat was packaged.

YEMENI ARCHITECTURE

"Occasionally, khat makes you crazy," chuckled our driver. "Sometimes men kill their friends and wives." I made a note to avoid making eye contact with anyone chewing even *gum* in the country. (Apparently the driver of the van in front of us was also indulging in the local treat because he drove off a curve and narrowly missed going over a steep cliff. His van abruptly stopped in a whirl of dust and its passengers jumped out and REFUSED to continue their journey until the driver was replaced. What became of those people is a mystery, as our vehicle slowly maneuvered around the commotion and continued its trek to the capital).

"Why would the government encourage people to use khat?" I asked our driver.

"Life is hard in Yemen," he responded. "The government is corrupt. People chew khat to forget their cares." And then, for emphasis, "With khat, people don't care about *anything*, including our leadership. So, the president condones khat and says it is okay, that it is as traditional in Yemen as tea."

* Costa Cruise Lines is the same Italian cruise line whose ship *Concordia* plowed into a reef off the coast of Tuscany in 2012, killing 32 passengers. Coincidentally, we had sailed on the *Concordia* shortly before that accident happened.

By the time, the caravan of seven vans reached the capital, it was late, Lalo and I had seen enough to know we would never return to Yemen. Sometimes in travel there are lands where you just instinctively know there is nothing that would ever lure you back. When our guide announced we would all have to check out of the posh hotel at 6:30 a.m. the following morning, we decided to abandon the tour, sleep-in late, and hire a private car and driver to take us to our cruise ship at a more civil hour. After all, this was supposed to be a vacation.

We realized halfway through brunch the next morning that neither of us remembered what time the ship was scheduled to depart Aden. Panic set in: was the reason the caravan departed so early due to the fact that the ship left at noon? It was 10:30 a.m. and the drive back to port would take at least two hours. All of our written material was left on board the ship--we did not even carry a phone number of the ground operator. The only stub I could find was a torn ticket with the words, "Scenic Sana'a—no return" printed above the Costa Cruise logo. It might as well have read, "Good Luck." Would we become permanent residents of this God-forsaken country?

We alerted the hotel concierge of our dilemma, paid our bill, and rushed to our room, where, bumping into each other and delirious, we frantically threw things into our overnight bags. Fortunately, our driver had arrived early. Barking at each other, we jumped into his sedan and sped away, leaving only blurry-eyed Yemenis chewing khat in our wake, scratching their heads.

Told of our situation, the driver we hired gunned his car and said, "I guess that means you don't have time to see the Old City." Sensing our recoil, he pushed the pedal. "People here don't have much," he said, as a goat leapt out of the trunk of a car in front of us. "They think all Americans are rich. Are you rich?" We assured him we were not and settled into our seats as he continued to enlighten us of all things Yemeni.

"This is a dangerous place," he said, waving his hand above the dashboard. "Osama Bin Laden lived here--his father was born in Yemen. You can buy any kind of weapon on every street corner-- guns, hand grenades, rockets. Anything you want. That's important, because people here hold grudges."

SUCH A FRIENDLY COUNTRY

"Grudges?" I gulped, looking at my watch. The driver explained how in the 19th century, a family's cow was stolen by the head of another clan and the bloody revenge that ensued.

"To this day, those two families still kill members of each other's." He shrugged. "All because of a stolen cow 200 years ago."

An hour into our drive we detoured onto a road that took us directly into the heart of a busy market. In a matter of seconds our sedan was surrounded by throngs of curious onlookers. With cupped hands, many peered into our luxury car. At this juncture in our story, it should be mentioned that men in Yemen wear curved daggers fastened onto their belts, "specially designed to cut the throats of infidels" reported our driver who casually chewed a toothpick, with one hand on the wheel. Lalo, being of Mexican ancestry, could pass as an Arab; but there was little doubt what country I, wearing a shirt purchased in Waikiki that portrayed hula dancers performing against a background of swirling hibiscuses, came from. I slunk down in my seat and could barely rasp, "Step on it. Please."

COWERING IN A CROWDED MARKET

Eventually, we made it back to Aden in time to board the ship. After we downed a couple of drinks in the Mariner's Lounge to calm our nerves, the captain (and later the CEO of Costa Cruises) got an earful from us, challenging the wisdom of including Yemen as a port-of-call on a pleasure voyage. We later found out that our cruise ship was the last to drop anchor there.

Kurt Vonnegut's belief that "bizarre travel plans are dancing lessons from God" took on new meaning, and next time we will sit one out before stepping onto that dance floor again.

NOT HAVANA GOOD TIME

- Notes from A.C.T.'s October 2017 Cuba trip

Now that Americans are allowed to travel to Cuba, Steve is anxious to promote the country as a *must-see* destination.

"It's like boarding a time machine and traveling back to 1959!" he explains to all who will listen. "The Cubans are friendly, literate, and anxious to interact with Americans." The best way to tour the island, he says, is not by bus (due to terrible infrastructure), but by ship. Steve should know—he has been there, and to that end, he has chosen an itinerary offered by Royal Caribbean International (R.C.I.) aboard the *Empress of the Seas,* which features three days in Havana, the capital (two nights, actually, because the ship leaves the island on Day 3, but when selling travel, one goes by "days," as it sounds like you're getting more for your buck*).

"Is that enough time, though, to see all the sights?" asks J.W., a 74-year-old widow. "Absolutely!" assures Kanold. "Everything that's worth seeing is within a half day's drive of Havana. Plus, remember: Key West is also a featured port. That means you get to see Hemingway's house in Florida *as well* as his home in Havana!" It matters not that Hemingway actually resided in a sleepy town called

Finca Vigia outside of Havana. J.W. and 41 others sign up for the 7-day cruise program, which is slated for the first week of October.

The $1695 vacation customized by A.C.T. ("The 'C' stands for customized!") features flights on United Airlines from Santa Ana, CA to Houston, where the plane connects before arriving in Tampa, boarding port for the *Empress of the Seas*. One pre-cruise night at the Doubletree Hilton Hotel there and the six-day cruise (five nights) complete the package. Before final payment is due, Tina Spencer—A.C.T. office manager—sends everyone a four-page newsletter that highlights all the fun experiences people can look forward to, from shipboard activities to exciting shore excursions and not-to-be-missed attractions in Havana. Tina knows that communicating with clients before the final balance is due results in fewer cancellations. At this time, everyone is on board. Dixie Kanold, sister of owner Steve Kanold, is assigned to be the A.C.T. escort. At one time Dixie taught high school Spanish, so her presence should be a comfort to all.

*Words matter when it comes to enticing seniors to book a trip. Decades of catering to them have taught me never to post these 10 words on promotional flyers:

10) Trek
9) Snowboarding
8) Rap
7) Scuba
6) Camping
5) Horseback
4) Roller coaster
3) Jungle
2) Midnight
1) Wet

There is an old saying, "We plan, and God laughs." Hurricane Harvey develops over the Atlantic on August 17 and before it is over two weeks later, it leaves both Key West and Havana inundated. "Not to worry," Steve says to worried clients when the phones start ringing. "We're monitoring the situation." That's the mantra travel professionals use when catastrophes strike. As the documentation meeting approaches, people become more skittish, peppering the staff with "What if" scenarios and threatening to cancel. Things get downright hostile at the meeting, after the cruise line announces that because of damage Key West suffered from Harvey, the ship won't drop anchor there.

"Key West is the *only* reason I signed up!" R.B. insists. (Yeah, sure).

"Cruise lines reserve the right to substitute other ports or cancel them outright," Kanold says, pointing to the terms and conditions on A.C.T.'s reservation form.

"This is beginning to sound like a devastation tour," R.K. huffs.

"Cancel Vern and myself. How much will we get back?"

"*Nada,*" Dixie responds.

"As long as United flies into Tampa, as long as the hotel is open, and as long as the cruise is operating, it is YOUR decision to cancel, not ours." The honeymoon Dixie has had with her travelers is over.

"Were you two aware," J.H. says, narrowing her eyes, "that today the State Department put out a warning to Americans—not an advisory, but a **warning**—NOT to travel to Cuba?"

Steve looks at Dixie, who shrugs. "No," he says, "I was not aware of that."

"So, you are going to *force* us to go, putting us in harm's way?!"

Oh dear. The program is unraveling, and so are our clients. Steve smells a lawsuit.

"Count me out," another couple says, slapping down their documents. "There's also Hurricane Irma on its way. And Jose after that!"

To make matters worse, five days later United inexplicably reroutes the group's return flight through Newark, rather than Houston. Three more people cancel. And then Steve gets a call from the Doubletree Hilton in Tampa: water from hurricane Harvey has been detected between the drywalls of the hotel, so the group will be moved to the Tampa Grand Hotel, around the corner. More grumblings when the remaining participants are notified.

"This trip is jinxed!" E.R. complains.

"What's next—locusts?" Kanold asks his sister.

One couple who had been born in Cuba cancels, saying traveling there now would put them at risk.

"Why?" Steve asks. "Cuba is not at war with any country. No one is bombing Havana."

"The U.S. Embassy was bugged. Too risky," says C.G., the wife. "We're not going."

Four days before the flight to Tampa, Royal Caribbean Cruises announces Key West has cleaned up its streets so that the ship will once again dock there. And Havana's flooding has ebbed. With trepidation, Dixie's reduced group of 32 travelers makes its way to Florida and embarks on its voyage. The ship is more than half empty, and the *Empress* staff is as anxious as its passengers.

"Nothing but wrong information, that's what the staff is giving us!" grumbled Dixie.

Bad guidance, but beautiful weather, it turns out, and much pampering by the crew of the ghost ship.

Hurricane Nate reaches the Gulf coast on October 7, the date Dixie's group returns to Tampa. For a time, Houston Airport is closed. Being diverted to Newark rather than connecting in Texas turns out to be a good thing. Meanwhile, back at home, the staff at A.C.T. has the unfortunate job of informing all those who opted not to go that cancellation insurance does not cover acts of God, like hurricanes. Furthermore, the A.C.T. team repeats over the phone what was said from the start: all aspects of the trip were operational—air, ground, and cruise. Steve doubts that those nine individuals who cancelled will ever book another tour with A.C.T.

"Shoot the messenger," he sighs, vowing never to offer another Caribbean cruise during hurricane season. "Let's now turn to our next vacation."

FRIENDLY CUBANS

THE TOAST OF HAVANA

THOUGHTS SUITABLE FOR POSTCARDS

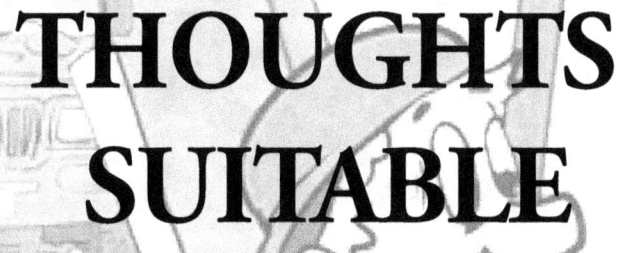

THOUGHTS SUITABLE FOR POSTCARDS

"Every trip has to end, but what a journey this has been!"
---Pre-engraved epitaph on Steve Kanold's cremation niche

Interned at Desert Memorial Park near Palm Springs, California are many celebrities who, in their sunset years, had retired to the desert for sunshine, golf, and solitude. Among them are Sonny Bono and Frank Sinatra who died, coincidentally, in the same year, 1998. Across the Park is Forest Lawn's Columbarium, a wall of cremation niches containing the ashes of Dinah Shore, Rock Hudson, Buddy Rogers, and a host of other stars. There will lie this writer's final resting place, along with his partner Lalo Alvarez's.

But it is Sinatra's most famous song, "My Way," that is of interest to me now; rather, there is a stanza in that tune which could very well be substituted for my own epitaph:

I've lived a life that's full
I've travelled each and every highway
And more, much more than this
I did it my way

And there's the rub—I did it my way, not Rick Steve's or Arthur Frommer's or Paul Theroux's or your way. I traveled my way, with prejudice in style and preferences, which is a subjective choice. And the fact that travel is subjective is the first of 20 summary points that will conclude this book:

1) <u>Travel, like everything else in life, is subjective;</u> that is to say, there is no right or wrong answer to questions like, "What is your favorite country?" It should be clear by now that you will like some destinations better than others—for me, the French Riviera beats the Gobi Desert; Italy over Scandinavia; South Africa over Tunisia, and *anywhere* over Belgium. I don't even like to recommend restaurants at my age, as I've had friends who return and moan, "You call *that* a good place to eat?" One person's experience is another's nightmare, whether it is a book, a movie, a meal, or vacation. Taste in travel is subjective. Next....

2) <u>Learn from the mistakes you've made on vacations.</u> I think of Otto Warmbier, the tragic young man who in 2015 was apprehended by the North Koreans for trying to steal a propaganda banner from his hotel. He was flown back in a comatose state and died soon afterward. That could have been me in 1972, when at 21 years old I foolishly pulled down a street sign bearing my name—*Kanoldstrasse*--off a pole in Soviet-Controlled East Germany to sneak home. What was I thinking?! Or the incident in Yemen, when Lalo and I failed to remember what time the cruise ship departed, described in this book's Exotic Destination chapter. I shudder to think of mistakes clients have made while touring (the guy we saved from falling over Victoria Falls, tourists who have opened their

wallets to gypsies, drunken adults who have almost toppled off the Leaning Tower of Pisa, saps buying time shares in a moment of passion, taking a walk with wild lions in Zimbabwe, etc.). Who says wisdom comes with age? *Learn* after such incidences, and once burned be twice shy.

3) <u>Solo travel</u>. There are a number of books on this subject, but it seems to me Socrates' famous line "Know thyself" summarizes it all. Do you enjoy your own company? If so, go it alone, because wonderful things can happen when you don't have a roommate or friend tagging along (suggested reading: Erica Jong's naughty "Fear of Flying"). Others go into complete panic mode when it comes to dining by oneself or lacking somebody to share experiences with, and you meet these poor souls with longing eyes and lonely faces all the time in foreign lands. On the other hand, singles can argue that many friendships are forged on tours and cruises. My opinion? If you travel solo but would like company, a smile goes a long way in attracting people and fulfilling that desire.

4) <u>Cultural understanding is important.</u> I wonder if "Holy cow!" originated in India. Instead of asking your guide why livestock is allowed to roam freely in the streets of New Delhi, remember that to Hindus, the beast may be someone's reincarnated relative. In China, spitting on the floor of restaurants and in streets, as disgusting as it is to westerners, is customary. Ditto, bowling to each other in Muslim countries is as common as shaking hands in America. Do a little research before leaving the comforts of home. I learned my lesson of cultural understanding while in southern France and in Bali (chapters 2 and 3).

5) <u>Running away from problems usually solves nothing</u>. If you have a bad marriage in Los Angeles, you'll have one in Cape Town 9,000 miles away and your attempt to rekindle the flame

will most likely fail. If you've lost a loved one, fleeing to Venice, Italy will make you feel sadder, not better. And traveling to *oui-oui Paree!* in search of the perfect French lover usually results in disappointment. (An A.C.T. female client—a librarian—was resolute in meeting Monsieur Right in the French capital and thought she nailed one before discovering over a candlelight dinner he was married with five children. Disheartened, she returned to her world of checkout cards and romance novels).

6) <u>Travel can be life transforming</u>. You will see your existence from new perspectives. Again, I point to books like "Seven Years in Tibet," "Eat, Pray, Love," "On the Road," and anything written by Bill Bryson or Paul Theroux. For me, visiting the Holy Land was transformative. A day before we went, a guide in Cyprus shared a drink with me and warned, "It matters not what religion you are, or even if you are an atheist or agnostic; but you will *know* that something very important happened there 2,000 years ago. The air is heavy with prayers." And she was right—I wept at almost every sacred site. As was my experience in Capri, Italy, Wordsworth's definition of poetry-- "the spontaneous overflow of powerful feelings" --could have easily been applied to that first life-changing trip to Israel. Has such an experience ever happened to you? It could occur by simply meditating on a pristine beach in the Seychelles, or staring in awe at the Grand Canyon for the first time. For many Americans, it has happened during a visit to Auschwitz or some other notorious concentration camp in Europe. Again, the answer is subjective—there is no right or wrong answer. You just know when it happens.

7) <u>Charting new territories—try it, you'll like it!</u> Yes, London, Paris and Rome are delightful cities, but so are Rangoon, Buenos Aires, and Sydney. Sometimes we get into a travel rut,

i.e., we keep returning to the same holiday spots, which is not particularly wise. "It's changed!" people often cry, meaning it's changed for the worse. Join the millions of travelers who pin flags onto their maps after experiencing *new* places. Friends, there are only two times in life: NOW and TOO LATE. You'll never have this time again! *Carpe Diem*—"Seize the Day," was first uttered by Horace, the leading Roman lyric poet during the time of Augustus. As the cliché says, life isn't a dress rehearsal—this is it! Don't put off that trip you desire, if you are now in shape to travel.

8) <u>From saints to whores</u>—Why do some travelers toss morality out the window while on vacation? We've noticed on trips that infidelity is common; married women who have ditched their husbands for a couple weeks' getaway have slept with rugged guides in Africa, and gay men on past tours have headed to bath houses almost as soon as their planes have landed in Bangkok. A number of females have made amorous advances toward our male escorts, and seemingly straight men have even sought liaisons with other guys on their holidays. We've seen it all. I am not a psychologist who can explain why they do it, but it is quite fascinating to see both reputable men and women ditch their halos in foreign countries. Could our company's name, *Adult* Customized Tours have something to do with it? I don't know, but the thought occurs: Would A.C.T. be liable if someone returned and spread a social disease to his or her partner, or if a "Fatal Attraction" scenario ensued? Have your lawyer call ours.

9) <u>Alex Haley's novel "Roots" was a bestseller in 1976 and told the story of Kunta Kinte,</u> an 18th century African who was captured as an adolescent and was sold into slavery after being transported to North America. Haley traced Kinte's life and

descendants down to himself. Ever since then, some people want to travel to Ireland to find their "roots," or to Belgrade (or other city) to retrace their family's "roots." Such journeys can be quite poignant as mine was when, in 1968, my father took my brother and me to the East German town of Apolda to view the gravestones of other Kanold family members. Our name was and still is a rarity, so to view a series of cemetery plots bearing "Kanold" had a startling and bonding effect on us. On that trip, we also traveled to the tiny Saxon village of Steinpleiss, where my paternal grandmother was born on the top floor of a farm house. Standing outside the dilapidated home with an old photo of the high window where the delivery took place, my father broke down after recognizing the site. Similarly, my mom cried when we took her to Kew Gardens in London; her mother used to play there as a child. Traveling and finding your roots is unlike any other life experience. Sadly, I have discovered that few millennials are interested in their family's genealogy and are unfamiliar with Haley's novel. Bye bye Miss American Pie....

10) <u>Great travelers are perennial students</u>. They love to learn and not just go along for the ride. They ask cogent questions of their guides, they research history in advance, and a few even take notes while on vacation —good ones, not just a list of what goes wrong, as globetrotters have a habit of doing. Great travelers are sponges of everything new! By leaving their country, these "students" also realize what it means to be an American. We live in the greatest, most free nation on earth and they return home having learned the same lesson that the children in Maurice Maeterlinck's novel "The Blue Bird" did, as well as the knowledge Candide gained in Voltaire's book of the same name, and what Dorothy became aware of at the end of "The Wizard of Oz"—that there is no place like home.

11) <u>Is there a difference between a tourist and a traveler?</u> *USA Today* predictably defines a tourist as someone who would carry "a camera, guidebook and map at all times and wear the same clothing he'd wear at home." A traveler, the newspaper continues, will "immerse himself in the local culture rather than standing out. If you're a traveler, you may try to explore the less-traveled areas and explore locations where tourism doesn't drive the economy. You'll interact with locals." In reality, I'm not sure there is a difference between the two, although travel snobs may sniff that they never want to be referred to as tourists. I embrace the following definition, posted on a website called the careerbreaksite.com: "A tourist tries foreign food but acts like he's putting a grenade in his mouth. A traveler eats the local food with abandon and spends the next 3 days on the toilet."

12) <u>Travel insurance is like any other type of protection coverage: It is an annoying expense until you need it</u>. That's about all I have to say about the subject, other than we advise people to review carefully the policy exclusions, like cancelling because of pandemics (usually not covered), pre-existing medical conditions, and so-called "acts of God" (read our chapter "Not Havana Good Time"). Cancel-for-whatever-reason insurance often costs twice as much as standard policies, and the carriers usually refund only 75% of a trip's cost. Finally, keep in mind that travel protection covers consumers before, during, and even after their vacation (i.e., if their luggage doesn't arrive home with them). For that reason, I recommend buying it, and any credible travel agent should at least offer it when people sign up for a trip, lest he be sued.

13) <u>Where are the happiest places in the world, outside of Disneyland</u>? Again, we revisit the word "subjective." *Forbes*

magazine each year publishes a list of "The Happiest 20 Countries in the World," and typically Scandinavian countries are in the top three: Finland, Denmark, and Norway. In 2020, Iceland—also a Scandinavian country --came in fourth and Switzerland ranked third. My best buddy in high school was an exchange student from Sweden (number 7 slot, right behind the Netherlands), and, after earning a doctorate degree in horticulture, unhappily had to sell vegetables each weekend in an open market to earn extra cash to offset Sweden's high taxes. If Scandinavia countries are the happiest (Google **Forbes Happiest Countries** to find how lists are tabulated), why is the suicide rate there so high? Just asking. My feeling is "happiness is where the heart is," whether it is in the slums of Mumbai or in posh Beverly Hills or at a Masai village in Kenya. Happiness is a state of mind, and I suspect there are plenty of unhappy people in the countries on the Forbes list. Anyone seen an Ingmar Bergman movie lately?

14) <u>Trains: ah, yes, Americans love choo-choo trains</u>, especially Californians, who are weary of driving freeways (the East Coast has plenty of trains, and riding them is no big thrill there). I have a funny rail story. On my first A.C.T. trip to China, at a time when there were more bicycles on the roads than cars— our group boarded an overnight train in Nanjing, capital of China's eastern Jiangsu Province, and traveled to Xian, where the famous Terra Cotta Warriors are displayed. The sleeping arrangements were crude, with two sets of bunk beds in each cabin accommodating a total of four passengers, and one toilet at the end of the car, equipped with "plumbing" that featured a hole in the floor boasting a view of the passing railroad ties. Care for a shower? Forget it—this was not the luxurious Orient Express. The ride to Xian, in the center of the country, was long and tedious. A college friend named Stan shared

my cabin and after a sleepless night in the cramped quarters, awoke feeling claustrophobic. He raised open the window, stuck his head out the fast-moving train and shouted, "I can't stand it any longer—I need to breathe!" At that very instant, someone two cabins forward tossed the contents of a piss pot out the window. Stan, in slow motion, pulled back his doused head, spitting and grabbing a towel in the process. Rack it up to "Learn from your mistakes while on vacation," number two on our summary list. The most *forgettable* train journey I ever took was one that everybody else in our group loved. It was a two-day ride aboard the Rocky Mountaineer Railroad from Banff, Canada to Vancouver covering over 500 miles, interrupted only by an overnight stay in Kamloops. The train slowly followed the same non-descript river for about 10 hours each day, and we passengers did nothing but eat and stare out windows. For me, the whole experience was akin to taking back-to-back international flights in coach class. As I mentioned, many loved the trip, so what do I know? Travel is subjective. Some people bought Edsels.

15) <u>Coronavirus, China, and the whole damned thing</u>. Covid-19 has decimated the travel industry. Am I telling you anything new? There will be years of analyzing the events of 2020, but we **do** know the virus came from China and the majority of immunologists believe China was aware of the outbreak months before the world did, yet did nothing to alert other countries and even continued sending people from Wuhan, the epicenter of the disease, to Europe and elsewhere. For that reason and others, including the fact that the Chinese steal intelligence from the U.S., suppress religions and even round up. Muslims and send them away in boxcars to internment camps; and for such horrendous things as butchering dogs and cats for meals.

A.C.T. will no longer offer "vacations" to China. (In Shijiazhuang, the capital of Hebei Province in northern China, dogs are thrown into cauldrons of boiling water alive). No longer will A.C.T. support with tourist dollars countries that engage in cruelty to humans and animals, and that spy and that deceive.

16) **<u>A few words on cuisine outside of the United States.</u>** We have mentioned prior to this point in the book how globetrotters complain about the lack of meatballs in Italy, and how Chinese food tastes as though everything is cooked in the same wok. Feedback (an appropriate noun) from our thousands of travelers on the subject of foreign food show a consensus that:

a) Mexican dishes are tastier and less heavy here than they are there.

b) German meals are heartier and richer in Deutschland than in Poughkeepsie, New York.

c) Vegetables in Africa, all organic, actually have *taste* to them. (as opposed to store-bought ones here in the states)

d) Australian dishes are as unappetizing as Britain's.

e) New Zealand needs to come up with something other than lamb.

f) You had better like sushi if you decide to tour Japan.

g) Cuisine on cruise ships is self-same and is by necessity unseasoned, regardless of how much you paid for the voyage.

h) South America is for carnivores.

i) Spanish food sucks. Mideast food? —the verdict is mixed.

j) Stick with seafood while in the Caribbean.

k) French food reigns supreme, from sauces to cheeses and desserts.

17) <u>We've expressed this earlier, but again: Two words can spoil a trip for travelers: Great expectations.</u> Often those who have preconceived notions of a destination are let down when they arrive. Conversely, we've heard over the years, "I never *expected* [such-and-such a place] to be so enjoyable!" Sometimes I think if people just go and let the magic of discovery happen, they will have a better time than researching months in advance. Who knew that there is a giant, 120-year-old Ferris wheel in Vienna? What a surprise to stumble across penguins in South Africa! Why, I had thought the Pyramids in Egypt were far away from Cairo—the pictures I saw didn't show how close they were to the city! Bora Bora is so different from Hawaii—where are the shops?! In travel, as in life, don't expect anything and you won't be disappointed.

18) <u>The cost of vacationing is often lowballed.</u> Usually, the price of a cruise is the cheapest part of one's voyage. Novices to cruising often forget that specialty restaurants and excursions and Internet usage are not included, let alone taxes and port fees. And when the ship drops anchor in its final harbor, guests are sometimes floored when their bar bill is presented to them. Ditto bus tours—the suggested tip to guides is $8-$10 a day, and don't forget the driver ($3-$5 per diem). "You didn't tell me!" globetrotters whine, feigning surprise. Yeah, whatever. Many countries are socialist, with prices are much higher than in capitalist America. Someone has to pay for those government subsidies. Almost every nation in Europe falls in the socialist category, so plan accordingly. I don't spend $100 a day on myself at home, but I budget that much when I travel. So should you! (On top of that, naturally, bring a credit card for the diamond you'll buy in Johannesburg, or for the opal ring you'll want in Sydney).

19) "<u>I'm fine. It's fine. Everything's fine.</u>" While that is the *attitude* to pack while traveling, most often we hear it shouted in lobbies when things are NOT fine from frustrated, usually exhausted clients, whose arms are flailing above them. When plans don't go right—when king beds aren't available in Mongolia, or the kitchen is out of morning prunes aboard a cruise ship, or the air conditioner is kaput in Casablanca, roll with it because really, what is the alternative? Take a deep breath and ask yourself, Will I remember this on my death bed? All of which brings us to our last thought suitable for a postcard.

20) <u>The cure for globetrots is easy</u>: Because attitude determines your altitude, relax and enjoy the proverbial ride. Shrug off delays, remember that what goes wrong rather than what goes right during a vacation makes a more interesting story when you get home, and know that this, too, shall pass. If you have a beef with your travel agent, postpone it until you return but be mindful of representations that were initially made. Were they met? If so, who cares if you had a miserable time—*you got what you paid for*. "Fun" is something you bring to the party and cannot be guaranteed by others. Finally, know when you should retire your passport. Some people feel the need to prove their mortality by flying to far off lands long after their prime.

ROCKY MOUNTAINEER RAILWAY: LIKE TWO BACK-TO-BACK INTERNATIONAL FLIGHTS

I end this chapter with a response I sent to a small group of country-clubbers who got together and complained about their trip to Africa, a summary of our positions and philosophy applicable to **every** A.C.T. travel program.

According to *Travel Agent Magazine*, globetrots affects only about 3% of travelers, and it has been an honor—a blessing, really—to have forged friendships with clients and to have experienced the wonders of the world with them. Funny…my customers thank *me*, when it should be the other way around. I was and still am truly grateful for their support and camaraderie. *Indeed, what a journey this has been!*

A.C.T.'s response to those complaining about their recent trip to Africa.

Group size: No promises were broken regarding the size of this group. Two buses, each with approximately 30 people (only 28 on the red bus!), were provided with its own guide/tour manager. Planes carry between 200 and 300 passengers (even more on the Emirate flights) and everybody on board must go through passport control, customs, and visa procedures. Therefore, delays at places like Nairobi Airport are inevitable and have nothing to do with A.C.T.'s group size. Those in the back of the plane would most likely be the last to be processed. This, savvy travelers realize, is a regrettable but inevitable fact on international trips. *Roll with it or rail against the wind.* "Blessed are the flexible, for they shall bend and not get out of shape."

"Holy Cow!" Oh wait, I'm in India. Sorry Grandma....

Namibia: On past trips, the village was alive with activity and the fact that few natives were present this year is regrettable. It is also a disappointment that no rhinos were spotted on the safaris, but again the fault is not A.C.T.'s, but poachers. Whether the issue is the paucity of animals or lack of villagers on any given day, some things are beyond the control of tour operators. Our responsibility is to see that the representations our company made are met, and to that end *every one we made—including a stop in Namibia—was achieved.* (To avoid the same incident happening again on Impalila Island, however, we shall amend future itineraries with "during your boat safari on the Chobe River, you will cruise the waters of Namibia" or "you will pass the country of Namibia").

Walking with the lions in Zimbabwe. What were you thinking – Whom would you sue -President Robert Mugabe?!

Guides: Like teachers, some are better than others. The same applies to travelers.

BEING BAPTIZED IN THE HOLY LAND'S JORDAN RIVER, A HIGHLIGHT OF MY LIFE

Nature of tourists: Too many people focus on what they are **not** getting on their vacations, rather than what they **are** getting for their money. **One should reflect on all the positive experiences!** While we *hope* our travelers enjoy the trips, they take with us, as long as A.C.T. delivers what is represented, "enjoyment" ultimately does not matter, as that—like "fun" --is subjective. People who say they would have gladly paid more for a smaller group most certainly would not have, as small-group operators like O.A.T. and Abercrombie and

Kent typically charge twice the price of A.C.T. (and in any case they do not offer a seven-country itinerary).

IF IT RAINS, THINK POSITIVE, BE CREATIVE AND SMILE! ZANZIBAR

Inconvenient truths: Some complainers drink too much alcohol and nurse hangovers throughout their vacations. Others have physical ailments, pop pills or have bad marriages, all of which affect their attitude and lead to chronic whining. After 42 years of customizing trips around the world, we have fortunately been confronted with just a handful of these bad apples and feel confident that our programs, which feature newsletters, documentation meetings, escorts,

special perks and quality hotels are unique in the industry, dollar for dollar. A.C.T. is proud of its legacy and—we repeat--as long as we deliver what was promised we sleep well, quite aware that travel isn't a beauty treatment (especially as one grows older) and that in the long run, delays at airports and snafus at hotel check-ins are hiccups that no one will recall when God summons him on that final, ultimate trip. Based on 40 years of feedback, it is our pampering which people remember and keeps them returning to A.C.T.

LIFE CHANGING: TOURING FORMER AUSCHWITZ CONCENTRATION CAMP IN POLAND.

EPILOGUE

EPILOGUE

"It's not where you go, but with whom"

- A.C.T. SLOGAN

I am grateful for the comments and suggestions made by friends who previewed this book. A special thanks goes to Janet Landfried, a wonderful editor and travel journalist, and of course my partner of 35 years, Lalo Alvarez who more than once gasped, *"You can't write that!"*

The slogan for A.C.T. came to me after our first dozen or so tours. Globetrotters notwithstanding, most who have traveled to foreign lands with our company have been happy, positive-thinking people, especially if they had never set foot in the destinations before. Escorting them was like taking kids to Disneyland for the first time. *<u>This</u>, I asked myself in disbelief, was what I got paid to do? How lucky can a guy get!* Many life-long friendships have been made on our tours, including two or three that have led to the altar. **To all who have traveled with Adult Customized Tours, I dedicate this book with heartfelt appreciation.**

I would be remiss to not express gratitude to current and past A.C.T. team members, all fine people who have worked in our office over the years and who have served as escorts. There are too many names to list, but suffice it to say that Tina Spencer, Linda Rose, and my sisters Kathy and Dixie deserve special recognition. Speaking of family, my late mother Barbara Soules, and her sister—my "Auntie Norma" --helped launch A.C.T. in its early days by soliciting activity directors at country clubs and stuffing envelopes, long before the Internet. Our company owes its success to them, as well as to Rosario Tachiquin, Lalo's mother who encouraged him to discover new lands, starting with the United States. At last count, Lalo has set foot in 132 countries.

Finally, what follows are select columns I wrote for newspapers, ending with one printed as a teenager in 1970 that was submitted from Bremen, Germany long before A.C.T. was founded. The others appeared in the *Hi Desert Star*, a hometown newspaper catering to California's upper desert communities, courtesy of the late Dr. Lou Gerhardt, pastor extraordinaire and sponsor of a weekly column titled "Tough Minded Optimism." Included is a touching travel piece Lalo wrote at Christmas, encompassing the "seize the moment" philosophy espoused in this book. Enjoy!

Barbara Soules

Rosario Tachiquin

TOUGH MINDED OPTIMISM
by Lou Gerhardt

Lalo Alvarez attends my Thursday seminars on positive living. He is vice-president of A.C.T. Tours and has visited more than 130 countries. I asked him to share this story.

When I came to America from Mexico, I knew I would not be able to go back and see my beloved mother until I got a Green Card, a legal process which would last 14 years. I spoke to her over the phone, of course, but I longed to hug her, to kiss her cheek and again taste her homemade Mexican food. Mom's tamales, especially, were delicioso. So when the Green Card finally arrived in early December, we both planned for my return to Mexicali, where I was raised. There was just one problem: I owned a store and could not leave until after Christmas.

My siblings had warned me that Mother was failing in health, but she assured me she was fine and eagerly looked forward to our reunion. On December 24, I packed the car with over $1000 in gifts—this would be one unforgettable fiesta!

Then the call came—Mom had been rushed to a hospital and physically died of a stroke shortly afterward. Shattered, I drove all night to Mexicali and joined my heartbroken family who had gathered to pay their final respects to the mother of 14 children. Afterward, when I was alone with my grieving father, he looked at the unwrapped gifts I had brought and said, "Your mother made you a present, as well, and left it in the kitchen." Inside the refrigerator was a plate of tamales, with a note attached that read, "Welcome home, my dear son Lalo. Feliz Navidad."

TOUGH MINDED OPTIMISM
by Lou Gerhardt

Adult Customized Tours (act-tours.com) is a long-established company owned by two residents of Yucca Valley, Steve Kanold and Lalo Alvarez, who attend my Thursday seminars on a regular basis. I asked them to comment on the travel industry.

"Here's a newsflash that probably won't surprise anyone over 50: after two decades of research, psychologist Dr. Thomas Gilovich of Cornell University in New York recently confirmed that the key to happiness is through experiences rather than material objects.

"We buy things to make us happy, and we succeed—but only for a while," Gilovich says. "New items are exciting to us at first, but over time the joy we derive from them dwindles. On the flip side, happiness that stems from things we've done actually goes up as time passes, because those experiences become a part of us and shape our identity."

Gilovich suggests that spending money on experiences like travel or new skills is a sounder path to happiness, because while new-fangled gadgets get old quickly, jaunts through Europe and elsewhere are still recalled often and fondly, years later.

"You can think that part of your identity is connected to material stuff," Gilovich explains, "but in fact those things remain separate from you. In contrast, your experiences really are part of you. We are the sum total of our experiences."

In summary, science now says it's totally ok to spend all your money on travel. And at A.C.T. Tours, we cannot agree more."

TOUGH MINDED OPTIMISM
by Lou Gerhardt

Steve Kanold has shared these reflections at my request. Read and enjoy.

"To celebrate my 64th birthday last month, I traveled to the Holy Land to be baptized in the Jordan River. Jesus said to enter the Kingdom of God, one must "be born of water" (John 3:5), and-- having never been baptized--I figured if not now, when?

Knowing little about the ritual, I phoned Reverend Lou Gerhardt, who has performed baptisms for over six decades, and asked if I should focus on my past discretions while being dunked, thereby drowning my sins (or at least sending them downstream).

"Heck no!" the good pastor retorted. "Go with a clear mind, embrace the setting and just appreciate the moment."

Good advice, I thought two weeks later, wading into the sacred river lined with Galilee pine trees. Dr. Lou was right--at this blessed place, nothing but joy could happen. My bliss was interrupted when suddenly I sensed nibbling at my toes. Carp were swimming between my feet! Other pilgrims felt them, too, as there was much fidgeting as the line made its way toward the minister who--waist high in water--seemed oblivious to the fish. By the time it was my turn, I was ready to leap into his outstretched arms. Like others who had gone before me, I pinched my nostrils and leaned back on cue, momentarily disappearing under the cool current. When it was over, I was relieved to step back onto dry soil. Annoyed that the ceremony had been upstaged, I nevertheless felt liberated and reborn. For the first time ever, I sensed that I had a shot of being admitted into heaven."

TOUGH MINDED OPTIMISM
by Lou Gerhardt

Adult Customized Tours (act-tours.com) is a long—established company owned by two residents of Yucca Valley, Steve Kanold and Lalo Alvarez, who attend my Thursday seminars on a regular basis.

I asked Steve to write the following brief essay.

"Recently, in just four days we went around the world on a Carnival Cruise ship. In that short time, we experienced five continents.

Our dutiful cabin steward, Sutinan, hailed from Bangkok, Thailand, in Southeast Asia. His colorful stories introduced us to his family, Thai food, tuk-tuks, and exotic floating markets.

A shy waiter, Anton transported us to his hometown of Brasov, Romania. Vicariously, through his tales we visited Dracula's castle in Transylvania and the People's Palace in Bucharest.

Kayla, which means "bright" in her native country of Botswana, brought breakfast to our room each morning and regaled us with memories of wild animals, the Chobe River, and African culture.

Every afternoon at happy hour we dropped anchor, so to speak, in Sydney, Australia, where that city's native son Liam poured us drinks at the ship's Violin Bar. Boy, did his vivid descriptions of local hangouts in the Land Down Under make us want to go!

Our chats with the pool attendant, Maria, from Peru reminded us of how much we loved that South American country. Homesick, she looked forward to returning to Lima and llamas after eight months at sea.

We didn't observe one other passenger interact with Carnival's international crew. Pity. Probably their focus was on the ship's two ports of call, Catalina and Ensenada."

With Local College Boys in Europe

By STEVE KANOLD

Steve and Norm Kanold and Marty Kay, formerly of Marina High, now Whittier, Redlands and UCI Students.

HUNTINGTON BEACH NEWS
THURSDAY, JULY 16, 1970

A few observations we have picked up from our European trip thus far: Swiss chocolate is not as good as See's candies from America. Beware when ordering rump steak in Europe—it is served rare unless otherwise specified. The major meal in Germany is served at lunch time. Only bread and butter with wurst and cheese for breakfast and dinner.

Ordering apple juice in a bar is just as common here as ordering beer. Germans do not say "Good morning" to one another on the streets unless they have previously been introduced.

Very little, if any, differences between first and second class compartments on European trains, which are always punctilious. Yodeling in Switzerland is primarily for tourists.

I'd hate to be a weatherman here. One moment it is raining, the next moment the sun is shining. Polaroid cameras never sease to amaze Europeans, even though their camera shops are full of them.

Cherries are a popular fruit in German. Drinking tap water is unheard of here. One buys carbonated spring water. Very seldom do you find hot/cold faucets here, just warm/cold.

Many hotels charge every time a bath is taken. In Cologne it cost us 75 cents per bath! Found this out when we had to pay the bill.

Gambling machines fill German bars. European bar rooms do not have the reputation that American pubs have. Ties are often worn by the men to these family gathering places and women are often seen playing cards over a glass of beer.

Many television shows here would be rated "R" by our movie standards...restricted...no person under 17 admitted. Woolworth stores have invaded Germany.

We have our Volkswagen camper now. The thing looks and runs great. We picked it up with little trouble in Wiedenbrook before we journeyed on to Bremen. So far the trip has been a ball with little "tiffs" occurring now and then, but we are all still speaking....little arguments that were expected concerning luggage, road directions, etc.

For example in traveling from Wiedenbrook to Bremen on the North Sea, Norm wanted to follow the road signs while Marty wanted to follow the road map. What resulted was a compromise. We wound up heading south for Rome.

Today I had my first lesson in driving the camper...ha ha! Have you ever traveled down the Autobahn backwards?

Will write from Denmark.

www.ingramcontent.com/pod-product-compliance
Lightning Source LLC
LaVergne TN
LVHW021713060526
838200LV00050B/2635